NETWORK MONITORING

ZABBIX, SOLARWINDS, SPLUNK, CACTI

4 BOOKS IN 1

BOOK 1
MASTERING ZABBIX: PROACTIVE MONITORING FOR MODERN NETWORKS

BOOK 2
SOLARWINDS UNLEASHED: ADVANCED IT INFRASTRUCTURE MANAGEMENT

BOOK 3
SPLUNK ESSENTIALS: REAL-TIME INSIGHTS FROM MACHINE DATA

BOOK 4
CACTI IN ACTION: VISUAL NETWORK MONITORING MADE SIMPLE

ROB BOTWRIGHT

Published by Rob Botwright
Library of Congress Cataloging-in-Publication Data
ISBN 978-1-83938-932-0
Cover design by Rizzo

Disclaimer

The contents of this book are based on extensive research and the best available historical sources. However, the author and publisher make no claims, promises, or guarantees about the accuracy, completeness, or adequacy of the information contained herein. The information in this book is provided on an "as is" basis, and the author and publisher disclaim any and all liability for any errors, omissions, or inaccuracies in the information or for any actions taken in reliance on such information. The opinions and views expressed in this book are those of the author and do not necessarily reflect the official policy or position of any organization or individual mentioned in this book. Any reference to specific people, places, or events is intended only to provide historical context and is not intended to defame or malign any group, individual, or entity. The information in this book is intended for educational and entertainment purposes only. It is not intended to be a substitute for professional advice or judgment. Readers are encouraged to conduct their own research and to seek professional advice where appropriate. Every effort has been made to obtain necessary permissions and acknowledgments for all images and other copyrighted material used in this book. Any errors or omissions in this regard are unintentional, and the author and publisher will correct them in future editions.

BOOK 1 - MASTERING ZABBIX: PROACTIVE MONITORING FOR MODERN NETWORKS

BOOK 2 - SOLARWINDS UNLEASHED: ADVANCED IT INFRASTRUCTURE MANAGEMENT

BOOK 3 - SPLUNK ESSENTIALS: REAL-TIME INSIGHTS FROM MACHINE DATA

BOOK 4 - CACTI IN ACTION: VISUAL NETWORK MONITORING MADE SIMPLE

Introduction

In the digital age, where every service, transaction, and communication relies on the availability and performance of interconnected systems, **network monitoring** has become a foundational discipline for IT professionals. Whether managing a small office network or a global enterprise infrastructure, the ability to observe, analyze, and respond to events in real time is essential for ensuring business continuity, user satisfaction, and operational efficiency.

This book, titled **Network Monitoring**, is your comprehensive guide to four of the most powerful and widely used monitoring platforms in the industry: **Zabbix, SolarWinds, Splunk**, and **Cacti**. Each of these tools offers a unique approach to monitoring, with distinct strengths, use cases, and deployment models. By examining them side by side, this book equips you with the knowledge to select the right tool—or combination of tools—for your environment and leverage them effectively.

The book is divided into four focused volumes:

- **Book 1 – Mastering Zabbix: Proactive Monitoring for Modern   Networks**
  Zabbix is a robust open-source monitoring solution known for its flexibility, scalability, and deep customization capabilities. This section dives into designing scalable architectures, configuring items and triggers, creating reusable templates, and setting up advanced alerting and automation workflows.

- **Book 2 – SolarWinds Unleashed: Advanced IT Infrastructure   Management**
  SolarWinds is a commercial solution renowned for its user-friendly interface and comprehensive suite of monitoring tools. This section explores its Orion Platform, Network Performance Monitor (NPM), alerting and reporting engines, and integrations for managing on-premises and cloud infrastructure alike.

- **Book 3 – Splunk Essentials: Real-Time Insights from Machine   Data**
  Splunk takes a different approach by focusing on indexing, searching, and visualizing unstructured machine data in real time. This section covers ingestion strategies, Search Processing Language (SPL), dashboards, alerts, and how to use Splunk for both operational visibility and security analytics.
- **Book 4 – Cacti in Action: Visual Network Monitoring Made   Simple**
  Cacti is a lightweight, SNMP-focused graphing tool perfect for visualizing bandwidth usage and device performance over time. This section guides you through installation, working with templates, polling, graph management, and scaling for large environments using plugins and automation.

Whether you're a network administrator, systems engineer, DevOps practitioner, or IT manager, this book offers practical, real-world guidance for building reliable, efficient, and responsive monitoring environments. Through hands-on examples, performance tuning tips, troubleshooting strategies, and integration scenarios, you'll gain the tools and confidence to take control of your infrastructure's visibility.

In a world where downtime can cost thousands per minute and blind spots lead to breaches or performance degradation, investing in the right monitoring strategy is not optional—it's mission-critical. This book is your roadmap to mastering the tools that make that strategy a reality.

BOOK 1
MASTERING ZABBIX
PROACTIVE MONITORING FOR MODERN NETWORKS

ROB BOTWRIGHT

Chapter 1: Getting Started with Zabbix: Architecture and Setup

Getting started with Zabbix requires a solid understanding of its architecture and core components, as this forms the foundation for successful deployment and operation in any network environment. Zabbix is an enterprise-grade open-source monitoring solution designed to track and visualize metrics such as CPU load, memory usage, network traffic, disk space, application performance, and more, across physical, virtual, and cloud-based environments. Its architecture is highly scalable and modular, which allows for flexible deployments ranging from small single-server setups to large distributed systems monitoring thousands of devices in real time.

At the heart of the Zabbix architecture is the **Zabbix server**, which acts as the central point of the monitoring system. It is responsible for collecting, processing, and storing monitoring data, executing checks, handling triggers, sending alerts, and managing configuration. The server interacts with various agents, proxies, and other components to gather data and provide a real-time view of the health of your infrastructure. Complementing the server is the **Zabbix database**, typically powered by MySQL, PostgreSQL, or MariaDB. This is where all configuration settings, collected metrics, events, and historical data are stored. Given the potentially high volume of incoming data, it is crucial to properly size and tune the database backend from the start, especially in larger environments.

The **Zabbix frontend**, a PHP-based web interface, allows administrators and users to configure the monitoring system, visualize data, create dashboards, manage hosts and templates, define triggers and actions, and access historical information. This frontend communicates directly with the Zabbix server and database, serving as the main control panel for the entire monitoring operation. Proper installation of prerequisites such as Apache or Nginx, PHP modules, and secure access controls is essential to ensure optimal performance and user experience.

Zabbix agents are small software components installed on monitored devices—such as Linux servers, Windows machines, or BSD systems—that collect local metrics like CPU usage, memory consumption, process activity, and more. Agents transmit this information to the Zabbix server or a proxy at regular intervals. They can operate in passive mode, waiting for requests from the server, or in active mode, where they initiate the connection and push data. This flexibility allows administrators to choose the method best suited to network topology, security requirements, and firewall constraints.

In distributed environments or large-scale networks, **Zabbix proxies** play a critical role in optimizing data collection and reducing the load on the central server. A proxy acts as an intermediary between agents and the server, collecting and preprocessing monitoring data before forwarding it to the server. This approach reduces network latency and improves efficiency when monitoring remote locations or segregated networks. Proxies also allow continued data collection even if the connection to the central server is temporarily lost, ensuring that no monitoring information is missed during outages or maintenance periods.

Before installing Zabbix, it is important to conduct a thorough assessment of your monitoring requirements, including the number and types of devices to be monitored, the expected frequency of checks, and the volume of data retention needed. These factors will directly influence your hardware and software choices, such as the size of the database, the number of CPU cores, memory allocation, disk I/O performance, and network throughput. It is also advisable to plan the deployment of proxies and agents in a way that balances performance with manageability.

The installation process of Zabbix typically involves setting up the server and database on a dedicated machine or virtual instance, followed by the deployment of the frontend and configuration of the web interface. Most Linux distributions provide Zabbix packages via their repositories, and the official Zabbix documentation offers detailed instructions for supported platforms. Once the packages are installed, a configuration file for the Zabbix server must be edited to specify database connection parameters, logging options, timeout settings, and other operational preferences. The database schema and initial data are then imported using the provided SQL scripts.

After the server is configured and running, the next step involves accessing the Zabbix web interface for the first-time setup. During this process, administrators define connection settings for the database, configure the default user account, and verify PHP environment compatibility. Upon successful login, the dashboard presents a high-level overview of system health, alerts, and host status. From here, users can begin adding hosts manually or by using discovery rules, applying templates, and setting up checks and alerts.

Templates are a key concept in Zabbix and help streamline monitoring configuration by grouping items, triggers, graphs, and applications into reusable units. By linking templates to hosts, administrators can apply a standard set of monitoring rules consistently across multiple devices. Zabbix ships with several built-in templates for popular systems such as Linux, Windows, MySQL, Apache, Nginx, and more, though custom templates can also be created to suit specific requirements.

Security is an important consideration from the beginning of a Zabbix deployment. Communication between agents and the server or proxies can be encrypted using TLS, which helps prevent unauthorized access and data tampering. It is also recommended to secure the web frontend using HTTPS, configure strong passwords, enforce user roles and permissions, and regularly update the system to patch known vulnerabilities. In environments with strict compliance requirements, auditing access logs and enforcing two-factor authentication can further enhance security.

Monitoring data collected by Zabbix can be viewed in multiple ways, including charts, graphs, screens, and dashboards. Users can configure custom dashboards to focus on specific parts of the infrastructure, display real-time metrics, visualize trends, and identify bottlenecks. Built-in features such as data aggregation, SLA reporting, event correlation, and capacity planning provide deeper insights into the long-term performance of systems. By leveraging these visualization tools, teams can detect anomalies early, reduce downtime, and improve service reliability.

As Zabbix continues to evolve with each release, it introduces enhanced features such as predictive functions, preprocessing options, high availability support, and improved APIs for integration with external tools like Grafana, Ansible, or ServiceNow. Being open-source, Zabbix also benefits from a vibrant global community, frequent updates, and a wealth of documentation, plugins, and user contributions. Starting with a clear understanding of its architecture and carefully planning the setup process lays a strong foundation for building a reliable, scalable, and efficient monitoring solution.

Chapter 2: Installing and Configuring the Zabbix Server

Installing and configuring the Zabbix server is a critical step in establishing a functional and reliable monitoring system. Before diving into the installation process, it is important to prepare the environment and choose the appropriate operating system, database backend, and web server that will host the Zabbix components. While Zabbix supports multiple platforms, it is most commonly deployed on Linux distributions such as CentOS, Ubuntu, Debian, or RHEL due to their stability and wide community support. The Zabbix server requires several components to function correctly: a web server (commonly Apache or Nginx), a database system (such as MySQL, MariaDB, or PostgreSQL), PHP, and the Zabbix server package itself. Ensuring that these dependencies are in place and properly configured is essential for a smooth installation.

To begin, the operating system should be fully updated with the latest security patches and kernel updates. After preparing the environment, the next step is to install the Zabbix repository that matches your operating system and desired Zabbix version. This repository contains the server, frontend, and agent packages and is available directly from the official Zabbix website. Once the repository is added, the package manager can be used to install the necessary components, typically including zabbix-server-mysql or zabbix-server-pgsql, zabbix-frontend-php, zabbix-apache-conf, and zabbix-agent. During installation, you may also need to install supporting software such as the PHP runtime and required

PHP extensions, including modules for database connectivity, sockets, gettext, mbstring, and others.

The database must be initialized before starting the Zabbix server. This involves creating a dedicated database and user with appropriate privileges. For MySQL or MariaDB, the process typically includes logging into the MySQL client, executing commands to create the database (commonly named zabbix), and assigning privileges to a user that the Zabbix server will use to interact with the database. After the database is created, the Zabbix schema, images, and initial data must be imported. These are provided as SQL files in the Zabbix server package directory and can be imported using the mysql command-line tool. The import process may take a few minutes, depending on the system's performance.

Once the database is initialized, the Zabbix server configuration file, usually located at /etc/zabbix/zabbix_server.conf, must be edited to reflect the correct database connection parameters. This includes specifying the database type, host, port, name, user, and password. Additional settings such as the location of log files, debug level, timeout values, and history storage configuration can also be adjusted here to suit your specific requirements. Ensuring the database parameters are correct is vital, as any misconfiguration can prevent the server from starting or result in connectivity issues.

After configuring the server, it is time to configure the Zabbix frontend, which allows you to manage and view monitoring data through a browser-based interface. The Zabbix frontend requires a properly configured web server and PHP environment. If Apache is being used, the relevant configuration files will be installed automatically along with the Zabbix frontend package. The PHP settings must be adjusted to meet Zabbix's requirements, such as increasing memory limits, setting the correct timezone, and ensuring that required modules are enabled. These settings can typically be found in the PHP configuration file, often located in /etc/php.ini or a PHP-specific Apache module directory depending on the distribution.

Once PHP is configured and the web server restarted, you can access the Zabbix frontend through a browser by navigating to the appropriate URL, usually http://your-server-ip/zabbix. The installation wizard will guide you through the initial configuration, including verifying PHP settings, entering database connection details, specifying the server name, and testing connectivity to the Zabbix server. If all steps are completed successfully, the installation wizard will finalize the setup, and you will be able to log in to the frontend using the default credentials (Admin with password zabbix). It is recommended to change the default password immediately after the first login to enhance security.

After logging in, one of the first tasks is to ensure that the Zabbix server process is running. This can be done using standard service management commands such as systemctl start zabbix-server and systemctl enable zabbix-server to ensure the service starts automatically on boot. You can verify that the server is running by checking the status with systemctl status zabbix-server or by inspecting the log file located at /var/log/zabbix/zabbix_server.log for any errors or warnings. If the log file indicates problems with database connectivity, missing files, or incorrect permissions, these issues must be addressed before proceeding.

At this stage, the system is operational but not yet monitoring any hosts. Before adding devices or services to monitor, it is a good idea to configure the Zabbix server for email notifications. This involves setting up a media type for SMTP, defining the email server parameters, and creating an action that sends alerts when triggers fire. Zabbix supports a wide variety of notification channels including email, SMS, webhook, and third-party integrations. By configuring notifications early, you ensure that the monitoring system can alert you as soon as any problems arise.

Additional tuning can be done to improve the performance and reliability of the Zabbix server. For larger environments, it is advisable to increase the number of pollers and other processes by modifying parameters such as StartPollers, StartIPMIPollers, StartTrappers, and CacheSize in the zabbix_server.conf file. These parameters control how many simultaneous checks Zabbix can perform and how much memory it can use to store configuration and trend data. Changes to this file require restarting the Zabbix server for them to take effect.

System monitoring agents should be deployed on the devices you wish to monitor, and the hosts can then be added to the frontend by specifying their IP addresses, agent ports, and associated templates. Zabbix provides a powerful and flexible templating system that helps apply a standard set of checks, triggers, and graphs across multiple hosts with minimal manual configuration. Once hosts are added and linked to templates, data collection begins automatically, and metrics will populate the frontend within minutes.

By completing these steps, the Zabbix server will be fully installed and configured, ready to monitor systems, network devices, and services, and provide visibility into the health and performance of your IT environment.

Chapter 3: Understanding Hosts, Items, and Triggers

In Zabbix, understanding how hosts, items, and triggers work together is essential for building an effective monitoring environment. These three components form the foundation of data collection, condition evaluation, and alerting. A **host** in Zabbix refers to any monitored entity, such as a server, network switch, database, application, or even a cloud service. Hosts can represent both physical and virtual assets and are used as logical containers that group related monitoring elements. Each host has attributes like a name, visible name, group membership, IP address or DNS name, interface type, and associated templates. Hosts are organized into **host groups** for easier management, access control, and visibility, especially in large environments where different teams are responsible for different sets of infrastructure.

Each host can have one or more **interfaces** depending on how monitoring is conducted. These interfaces include agent interfaces, SNMP interfaces, IPMI interfaces, and JMX interfaces. The type of interface determines how Zabbix communicates with the host and what kind of data it can retrieve. For example, the Zabbix agent interface is used to collect local metrics like CPU usage, memory load, or running processes, while SNMP interfaces are often used for networking equipment like routers and switches. A host can have multiple interfaces defined, allowing for hybrid monitoring approaches that combine agent-based and agentless methods.

Within each host, **items** define the actual data points that Zabbix collects. An item specifies what to monitor, how frequently to check it, and what method to use. Items have several key properties, including a name, a key (which is a unique identifier for the metric), a data type (such as numeric, text, or log), update interval, history and trend storage duration, value units, preprocessing steps, and triggers that may depend on the item's data. For instance, an item might be configured to collect the system's free disk space every 60 seconds, store raw values for 90 days, and use a trigger to generate an alert if disk space falls below 10%.

Items can be either **passive** or **active**. Passive items rely on the Zabbix server or proxy to request data from the host agent, whereas active items involve the agent pushing data to the server at regular intervals. Active items are particularly useful in firewall-restricted environments where inbound connections are blocked. Zabbix supports a wide range of item types beyond the standard agent check, such as SNMP, HTTP, external scripts, user parameters, IPMI, and JMX, enabling it to monitor virtually any type of system or application.

To facilitate efficient management and consistency, Zabbix makes extensive use of **templates**, which are reusable sets of items, triggers, graphs, and applications that can be linked to multiple hosts. This approach allows you to define monitoring logic once and apply it to hundreds or thousands of similar hosts, such as all Linux servers, database servers, or switches from the same vendor. Templates streamline configuration, simplify updates, and help ensure uniformity across the infrastructure. When you link a template to a host, all the items and triggers in that template are automatically assigned to the host, reducing manual setup and risk of misconfiguration.

Triggers are logical expressions that evaluate the data collected by items and determine whether a specific condition has been met. When a trigger expression evaluates to true, it generates a problem event. When the condition returns to normal, the trigger changes state and generates a recovery event. Each trigger includes an expression that references one or more items, a severity level (ranging from "Not classified" to "Disaster"), and an optional description or comment. For example, a simple trigger might check whether CPU load exceeds 90% over a five-minute period, while a more complex trigger could combine multiple conditions such as high CPU load, low available memory, and excessive disk I/O.

Trigger expressions use a combination of **item keys**, logical operators, functions, and time-based calculations. For example, the function last() returns the most recent value of an item, avg() calculates an average over a defined period, and nodata() detects when an item stops collecting data altogether. These functions allow for precise control over when alerts are generated and help avoid false positives. Zabbix also supports trigger dependencies, which allow you to suppress alerts for related problems when a more fundamental issue is already acknowledged. For instance, if a host becomes unreachable, other triggers such as service failures on that host can be configured to depend on the availability trigger, thereby reducing unnecessary noise in alerting.

Each trigger can be associated with **actions**, which define what should happen when a problem or recovery event occurs. Actions can include sending notifications via email, SMS, or webhook; executing remote scripts; changing host status; or creating incidents in ITSM platforms. Actions can be customized with conditions based on trigger severity, host group, maintenance status, time of day, and other factors. Zabbix also supports **escalations**, which allow actions to follow a defined sequence, such as notifying a junior admin first, and escalating to a senior engineer if the problem persists.

In addition to being tied to triggers, items and their values can be visualized in multiple ways. Graphs provide real-time and historical views of item data, while screens and dashboards allow users to build composite views with multiple widgets, such as graphs, maps, data tables, clocks, and SLA indicators. These visual tools are essential for understanding the behavior of systems over time and for presenting data in a way that supports operational decision-making. Items can also be grouped into **applications**, which are logical groupings used primarily for organizational purposes in the frontend. For example, items related to disk usage, memory usage, and CPU load can be grouped under an application called "System Resources."

Zabbix also includes **low-level discovery (LLD)**, a powerful feature that automates the creation of items, triggers, and graphs based on dynamic data from hosts. For instance, if a server has multiple network interfaces or mounted filesystems, LLD can automatically detect and begin monitoring each one without requiring manual configuration. LLD rules can be defined within templates and are based on discovery rules, filters, and prototypes. This makes it especially valuable in dynamic environments such as cloud infrastructure, where hosts may change frequently or have non-uniform configurations.

By thoroughly understanding how hosts serve as the foundation for data collection, how items define what is being monitored, and how triggers determine when a condition requires attention, administrators can design highly responsive and intelligent monitoring systems. This trio—hosts, items, and triggers—is the backbone of Zabbix, enabling comprehensive visibility and alerting across diverse IT environments.

Chapter 4: Designing Templates for Scalable Monitoring

Designing templates for scalable monitoring in Zabbix is one of the most powerful ways to manage large infrastructures efficiently and consistently. Templates serve as reusable containers that hold monitoring logic, including items, triggers, graphs, discovery rules, and other elements that can be applied to multiple hosts. This allows administrators to define a set of monitoring rules once and deploy them across dozens, hundreds, or even thousands of hosts without needing to configure each host individually. In environments with dynamic or growing systems, such as cloud platforms, virtualized networks, or large enterprise infrastructures, templates are not just a convenience but a necessity for maintaining consistency, reducing errors, and simplifying configuration management.

The starting point for designing a scalable template is identifying the common characteristics shared by a group of systems. For example, all Linux servers might require monitoring for CPU load, disk usage, memory consumption, and system uptime. Similarly, all MySQL servers may need monitoring of query performance, buffer pool size, replication lag, and connection counts. Templates are most effective when they are built around shared functions or roles rather than specific devices. This abstraction allows for modularity and reuse, making it easier to adapt to changes in infrastructure over time. Instead of designing separate templates for each server, you can create layered templates: one for general OS-level metrics, another for role-specific monitoring, and a third for application-specific parameters.

Zabbix supports template linking, which means one template can inherit the contents of another. This is useful for building a hierarchy of templates where base templates define common items like ICMP ping or system load, and child templates add more specific checks like database health or web service availability. This hierarchical approach increases maintainability and reduces duplication, since changes made to the base template automatically propagate to all linked templates and the hosts they are applied to. When creating such a structure, it is important to avoid circular dependencies or overly complex nesting, which can make troubleshooting and updates more difficult.

Each template contains **items**, which define the actual data to be collected. When designing items in templates, it is crucial to use consistent naming conventions and clear descriptions, as this improves readability and usability later. For example, an item collecting CPU load might be named "CPU Load (1 min average)," and use a key such as system.cpu.load[percpu,avg1]. Carefully chosen intervals for data collection also matter, since collecting data too frequently may overload the system and the Zabbix server, while collecting too infrequently can cause blind spots in monitoring. Templates should balance granularity with performance, ensuring that essential metrics are collected often enough to allow timely alerts without creating unnecessary load.

Templates also include **triggers**, which evaluate the data from items and determine when something abnormal is occurring. When creating triggers in templates, it is best to design them with flexibility and scalability in mind. Using macros within triggers allows you to parameterize thresholds per host without modifying the template itself.

For instance, instead of hardcoding a value like 90% for CPU usage, you can use a macro like {$CPU_WARN} and define that macro individually for each host. This allows the same template to be reused across systems with different performance profiles. It also centralizes configuration, which makes future updates easier to manage.

Macros in templates extend beyond trigger thresholds. They can be used to define SNMP community strings, authentication tokens, script paths, or any other variable values that might change per host or group. Zabbix supports macros at several levels, including global, template, host, and user macro levels. Understanding the macro resolution order is essential for avoiding confusion, especially when multiple layers of macros are used. Documenting macro usage within template descriptions helps prevent misconfiguration and makes it easier for teams to collaborate on template maintenance.

In addition to items and triggers, templates can include **graphs** for visualizing data. While graphs in modern versions of Zabbix are increasingly replaced by widgets in custom dashboards, traditional graphs can still be useful for quick analysis of single host performance. When designing template-based graphs, selecting the right items to include and choosing meaningful titles and units improves usability. For example, a graph showing "Memory Usage" might include items for total memory, used memory, and cache, each with distinct colors and labels. Though templates apply the same graph to all hosts, the data displayed is always host-specific, enabling scalable and uniform visualizations.

Templates also support **low-level discovery (LLD)**, which is indispensable for environments where the number or type of monitored entities varies between hosts. LLD can be used to discover filesystems, network interfaces, mounted disks, running services, or even virtual machines. Discovery rules are defined within templates and specify how to obtain the list of monitored items dynamically. Item, trigger, and graph prototypes are then created based on these discovery results. For instance, an LLD rule for disk partitions might use the key vfs.fs.discovery to automatically detect all mount points on a system. Corresponding item prototypes would collect usage statistics for each mount point, and trigger prototypes could generate alerts if usage exceeds a certain threshold.

Proper use of filtering within LLD rules ensures that only relevant entities are monitored. For example, you may not want to monitor pseudo filesystems or temporary mounts, so you can define filters that exclude paths like /tmp or /dev. This improves the signal-to-noise ratio and avoids unnecessary data collection. Since LLD-based monitoring adapts automatically as systems change, it is particularly valuable in cloud-native and containerized environments where components frequently appear and disappear.

When designing templates for scalability, it is essential to consider naming standards, documentation, and change management. All templates should have clear and descriptive names that reflect their purpose, such as "Template OS Linux," "Template App Apache," or "Template DB MySQL." Descriptions within the template should explain what the template monitors, what dependencies it has, what macros are required, and any caveats for use. Version control systems can be used to track changes to templates, especially in large teams or environments with strict compliance requirements. Exporting templates as XML and storing them in a repository enables rollback and peer review, helping prevent unintentional changes that could affect hundreds of hosts.

Zabbix also allows for importing and exporting templates through the web frontend or the API. This means that templates can be shared between environments or even downloaded from the Zabbix community and vendor repositories. When importing third-party templates, it is recommended to review and adapt them before use to ensure compatibility with your naming conventions, thresholds, and organizational policies. Over time, your template library will grow to reflect the specific needs of your organization, serving as a centralized and standardized way to enforce consistent monitoring practices across the board.

Well-designed templates improve scalability, reliability, and operational efficiency by ensuring that every monitored system adheres to a predefined set of rules and alerting standards. This reduces configuration drift, enhances visibility, and simplifies onboarding new systems into the monitoring ecosystem. The more thought and structure you apply to template design, the more value Zabbix can deliver across your infrastructure.

Chapter 5: Advanced Notifications and Escalation Rules

Advanced notifications and escalation rules in Zabbix form a critical part of any serious monitoring strategy, enabling teams to respond swiftly to issues, prioritize critical events, and reduce response time across all layers of infrastructure. While Zabbix is well known for its powerful data collection and visualization capabilities, its alerting and escalation engine is equally robust and customizable, offering deep integration with operations workflows and team structures. At the core of the notification system are **actions**, which define what should happen when certain conditions are met, such as a trigger changing its state from OK to PROBLEM or from PROBLEM to OK. An action typically consists of an operation or a series of operations, such as sending a message, executing a remote command, or even disabling a host.

To create an effective notification strategy, it is important to start with **media types**, which are the channels through which messages are delivered. Zabbix supports a variety of built-in media types, including email, SMS, Jabber, and webhook. Each media type can be customized with parameters such as SMTP servers for email or API endpoints for webhooks. Starting with Zabbix 5.x and continuing into later versions, the webhook functionality has expanded significantly, making it possible to integrate with third-party services like Slack, Microsoft Teams, PagerDuty, Opsgenie, and many others through ready-made or custom webhook templates. Each media type defines the method and format of communication, and multiple media types can be assigned to the same user depending on their preferences or role.

Once media types are configured, individual **users** must be assigned with appropriate media settings. Each user can specify one or more delivery methods, set a severity threshold for messages they are willing to receive, and define the active time period during which they want to be notified. This granularity makes it possible to build notification policies that respect working hours, roles, and escalation hierarchies. For instance, a level-one technician might only receive alerts during working hours and for low- to medium-severity problems, while senior engineers may be on-call 24/7 and handle high-severity alerts. Defining user groups and linking them to action conditions allows for fine-tuned targeting of messages without manually maintaining recipient lists for every new alert.

Actions are the primary mechanism for triggering notifications, and they consist of conditions and operations. Conditions determine whether the action will be executed, based on factors such as trigger severity, trigger name, host group, host name, maintenance status, or even tags. Tags are a powerful feature in modern Zabbix versions and are used to categorize events more flexibly than traditional host groups or names. By using tags in triggers and defining tag-based conditions in actions, administrators can easily route alerts based on the nature of the issue, such as tagging events with type=database or service=http. This allows alerting logic to be decoupled from rigid host structures and adapt more readily to changing environments.

Operations define what actually happens when an action is triggered. A simple operation might be sending a message to a user group via email, while more complex operations could include running a remote script to restart a failed service or update a ticket in an ITSM platform. Operations can be repeated, delayed, and executed conditionally. For example, you can configure an operation to send an initial alert to a junior administrator immediately when a trigger fires, then escalate the issue to a senior engineer if the problem persists for 15 minutes. This brings us to the concept of **escalation steps**, which allow actions to progress through multiple stages based on time or the number of attempts.

Escalation rules are configured as part of action operations and are key for managing critical issues that require timed responses. Each escalation step can include a different set of operations, delays, or recipients. By assigning steps to different time intervals, Zabbix allows you to create workflows that mimic real-world support escalation processes. For example, if a server becomes unresponsive, the system can send a message to the primary on-call engineer within the first minute. If no acknowledgment or resolution occurs within ten minutes, the next step can notify a team lead or manager. Further delays might include engaging an external support vendor or triggering automated remediation tasks.

Zabbix also supports **acknowledgments**, which are manual actions taken by users to indicate they are aware of a problem. An action can be configured to react differently depending on whether a problem has been acknowledged. This makes it possible to prevent escalation if someone is already addressing the issue or to escalate more aggressively if no one responds. For example, you can configure an operation that only triggers after a certain amount of time has passed *without* acknowledgment, ensuring that unresolved problems do not fall through the cracks.

Maintenance periods can be defined to suppress notifications during planned downtimes or maintenance windows. These periods can be one-time or recurring, and when a host or group is in maintenance, triggers may still change state and log events, but notifications and actions can be skipped based on the configured type of maintenance. This is particularly helpful during patch cycles, system upgrades, or testing periods, when alerts would otherwise create unnecessary noise. Proper use of maintenance windows ensures that notification systems remain meaningful and trustworthy to the recipients, avoiding alert fatigue.

In more complex environments, actions can also be combined with **remote commands**, allowing Zabbix to respond to problems automatically. For example, if a web server is detected as down, Zabbix can attempt to restart the service automatically before sending any notification. These commands are executed by the Zabbix agent or proxy, depending on the architecture, and can include any shell command, script, or automation playbook. While powerful, remote commands must be used cautiously and should include proper error handling and logging to ensure traceability.

The recent enhancements to the Zabbix API also make it possible to create, update, and manage actions programmatically. This enables integration with CI/CD pipelines, configuration management tools, and custom dashboards. Teams can automate the creation of notification policies or dynamically assign media types based on infrastructure changes. For example, a newly provisioned host can automatically inherit notification logic through a templated approach, using tag-based discovery and predefined action logic.

Advanced notifications and escalation rules in Zabbix provide a flexible, granular, and powerful alerting framework that can be tailored to match the organizational hierarchy, operational responsibilities, and urgency of different system events. By leveraging media types, user roles, trigger tags, escalation steps, and maintenance windows, Zabbix enables a proactive monitoring environment where alerts are not only timely but also intelligent, reducing mean time to response and improving overall system reliability.

Chapter 6: Visualizing Data with Dashboards and Maps

Visualizing data with dashboards and maps in Zabbix is a fundamental aspect of transforming raw metrics into meaningful insights that support operational awareness, capacity planning, and incident response. While data collection and alerting provide the foundation for any monitoring system, visualization is what allows users to interpret trends, identify anomalies, and communicate system health to both technical and non-technical stakeholders. Zabbix offers a wide range of built-in tools for visualization, including modern, customizable dashboards, legacy screens, traditional graphs, and highly interactive network maps. These elements work together to present information in real time, making it easier for teams to act quickly and efficiently when issues arise.

The **Zabbix dashboard** is the primary visualization interface and is designed to be both flexible and dynamic. Each user can create personalized dashboards that reflect their specific role or area of responsibility, such as server monitoring, network performance, or application health. Dashboards are made up of **widgets**, modular components that display various types of information, such as graphs, problems, discovery statuses, top hosts by load, service status, data overviews, text notes, and more. Widgets can be resized and repositioned via a drag-and-drop interface, making it easy to construct layouts that suit the needs of NOC teams, system administrators, or application developers.

Widgets can be configured to show real-time data or aggregated trends over specific time ranges. For instance, a CPU usage graph for critical servers can be set to display the last 30 minutes for immediate performance feedback or the last 7 days to reveal longer-term trends. The **Problems widget** is one of the most widely used elements, showing active alerts with options to filter by severity, host group, tags, or acknowledgment status. This widget enables teams to see at a glance what needs immediate attention and who is responsible for resolving each issue. Other useful widgets include the **Top hosts widget**, which ranks systems by metrics such as CPU load or network traffic, and the **Trigger overview**, which provides a matrix view of trigger states across many hosts.

Permissions in Zabbix dashboards are tightly integrated with user roles and host group access. This means that different teams can build dashboards that only display data relevant to their responsibilities, maintaining data confidentiality and avoiding clutter. A database team might have a dashboard showing replication lag, query throughput, and buffer pool usage, while a networking team focuses on interface errors, bandwidth consumption, and SNMP link status. Dashboards can be shared globally, assigned to user groups, or kept private, depending on how they are intended to be used. The ability to clone and export dashboards also makes it easier to standardize visualizations across multiple environments or departments.

In addition to modern dashboards, Zabbix continues to support **classic screens**, which are legacy visualization tools that allow users to create fixed grid layouts of graphs, maps, plain texts, or other widgets. While screens lack some of the flexibility of dashboards, they remain useful for building large overview pages or NOC-style display boards that show the status of multiple services or systems side-by-side. Screens are especially valuable when designed for wall-mounted monitors, where operators need to observe a broad array of metrics at all times without navigating between pages.

Another powerful visualization feature in Zabbix is the **graph widget**, which provides detailed views of historical data. Graphs can be single-item or multi-item, and they support features such as color customization, legend display, min/max values, and selectable time ranges. While Zabbix automatically creates graphs for many item types, custom graphs can also be defined within templates or directly on hosts. Multi-item graphs are particularly helpful for comparing related metrics on the same chart, such as incoming and outgoing network traffic, or used versus total memory. These comparisons make it easier to identify correlations and root causes of performance degradation.

Zabbix also includes **network maps**, which offer a highly visual and interactive way to represent the topology of your infrastructure. Maps are composed of elements like hosts, host groups, triggers, or custom shapes and links that can show the relationships and dependencies between various components of the IT environment. Each element on the map can change color or display an icon based on its status, such as turning red when a host is down or flashing if a trigger is active. This makes maps ideal for real-time operations monitoring, where teams need to see the big picture of their network and quickly isolate trouble spots.

Maps can be static, manually created with fixed elements, or **automated through map discovery**, where components are added based on LLD or service discovery rules. Zabbix maps also support **link indicators**, where the status of the connection between two nodes is based on specific triggers or item values, such as packet loss or latency thresholds. These visual cues help detect degraded service paths or segment-specific problems. Users can embed maps into dashboards or open them as full-screen views for control room displays.

Zabbix also supports **geographical maps** through integration with third-party tile services like OpenStreetMap. With this functionality, hosts can be placed on a real-world map using latitude and longitude coordinates, and their status is reflected visually through color-coded icons. This feature is especially useful for organizations managing dispersed infrastructure, such as telecommunications providers, logistics companies, or emergency services. By overlaying monitoring data on a real-world map, it becomes easier to identify regional outages, infrastructure strain, or environmental impacts.

To enhance visualization even further, Zabbix provides **graph prototypes** tied to low-level discovery rules. These allow for automatic generation of graphs based on dynamically discovered entities like disk partitions, network interfaces, or Docker containers. When a new instance is discovered, Zabbix can automatically begin collecting data and generate appropriate visual representations without manual intervention. This feature dramatically reduces setup time in dynamic environments and ensures consistency across hosts with varying configurations.

Zabbix also supports exporting data to external visualization platforms such as Grafana, which can connect via the Zabbix data source plugin. Grafana adds further flexibility with its wide range of chart types, advanced filtering, and cross-panel correlations. For teams already using Grafana for other data sources like Prometheus or Elasticsearch, integrating Zabbix into a unified observability dashboard can provide greater context and operational value.

Through the combination of dashboards, maps, graphs, screens, and external integrations, Zabbix offers a rich and versatile suite of visualization tools that adapt to the needs of small teams and enterprise-scale operations alike. These tools not only provide visibility into infrastructure health but also support long-term planning, audit compliance, and business continuity efforts. Whether it's a single server or a globally distributed network, visualization is what turns data into action.

Chapter 7: Agent vs Agentless Monitoring: Best Practices

In Zabbix, monitoring can be performed through both agent-based and agentless methods, and understanding the differences between the two approaches is essential for designing a reliable, scalable, and secure monitoring strategy. Each method comes with its own strengths, limitations, and ideal use cases, and often the most effective solution is a hybrid one that combines both techniques to cover a wide range of systems and devices. Zabbix agents are lightweight programs installed on the target systems, enabling the collection of local data that is otherwise inaccessible or limited via remote means. Agentless monitoring, on the other hand, relies on standard protocols such as SNMP, IPMI, HTTP, SSH, WMI, or custom scripts to gather data without requiring any software installation on the monitored system.

Zabbix agents are available for a wide range of operating systems, including Linux, Windows, macOS, BSD, and others. The agent communicates with the Zabbix server or proxy to provide real-time metrics such as CPU usage, disk space, memory consumption, process status, log entries, and custom application data. One of the key advantages of agent-based monitoring is its depth of visibility, as it can access internal system statistics and configuration data with minimal performance overhead. Agents can be configured to run in passive or active mode. In passive mode, the Zabbix server or proxy initiates the connection and requests data. In active mode, the agent connects to the server or proxy at regular intervals and sends predefined metrics. Active mode is particularly useful when the monitored host is behind a firewall or does not allow inbound connections.

Agent-based monitoring provides several benefits, including low network usage, granular control over what data is collected, and support for custom user parameters. These parameters can be configured on the agent host to extend its capabilities and monitor application-specific values, execute scripts, or fetch results from external sources. For example, you can configure an agent to monitor the number of active sessions in a custom web application or the status of a database replication process. Agents also support secure communication through encryption, ensuring that data transmitted between the monitored host and the Zabbix server is protected against interception or tampering.

However, agent-based monitoring also has certain limitations. Installing and maintaining agents across a large number of hosts can become a logistical challenge, especially in environments where system access is restricted or managed by third parties. Additionally, agent updates and configuration changes must be managed centrally, often requiring configuration management tools or automation frameworks to ensure consistency and compliance. In some organizations, deploying third-party software is not permitted on production systems due to security policies or vendor restrictions, making agentless methods the only viable option.

Agentless monitoring in Zabbix fills this gap by enabling data collection through standard remote protocols. SNMP, or Simple Network Management Protocol, is one of the most commonly used agentless methods and is especially prevalent in network hardware such as routers, switches, firewalls, and printers. SNMP operates using a request-response model, where the Zabbix server or proxy queries predefined OIDs (Object Identifiers) to retrieve system statistics like interface status, packet errors, and CPU temperature. SNMP can be used in both polling and trap modes, allowing Zabbix to either actively request data or passively receive notifications when certain conditions are met.

Another popular agentless method is WMI, or Windows Management Instrumentation, which is designed for monitoring Windows-based systems. WMI allows administrators to collect data on system performance, software inventory, running processes, and configuration settings without installing any software on the target machine. Zabbix can perform WMI queries using remote checks configured within the host interface. However, WMI-based monitoring tends to be more resource-intensive than agent-based alternatives and may experience latency or timeout issues in larger environments.

For secure and controlled remote access, Zabbix supports SSH-based monitoring, where custom scripts can be executed on remote Linux or Unix systems over an encrypted channel. This is useful for running ad-hoc checks or accessing metrics not exposed via SNMP or standard agents. Similarly, HTTP-based checks allow Zabbix to interact with web APIs and endpoints, enabling the monitoring of application health, response time, and service availability. By using HTTP GET or POST requests and evaluating return codes or content patterns, Zabbix can effectively monitor RESTful services or public websites.

When deciding between agent and agentless monitoring, best practices involve evaluating the nature of the target system, the level of detail required, security considerations, and ease of maintenance. For systems under direct administrative control and requiring deep-level metrics, agents are usually the best choice. For third-party systems, embedded devices, or restricted environments, agentless approaches offer a practical alternative. In most environments, a hybrid approach offers the greatest flexibility and resilience, enabling comprehensive coverage while minimizing overhead and administrative burden.

One of the most effective ways to manage a hybrid monitoring environment is by using templates tailored to specific data collection methods. Zabbix allows the creation of separate templates for agent-based and SNMP-based monitoring, each containing appropriate item keys, triggers, and graphs. These templates can then be linked to hosts according to their monitoring method. For example, network switches may be linked to SNMP templates, while application servers use agent-based templates with additional user parameters. This modular approach promotes reusability and consistency across the monitoring infrastructure.

Monitoring performance and scalability should also be considered when mixing agent and agentless methods.

SNMP polling can place load on both the Zabbix server and the monitored devices if not configured properly. To avoid excessive traffic and data collection delays, administrators should fine-tune polling intervals, avoid redundant checks, and distribute load across proxies when needed. The use of preprocessing rules in item configuration can also help reduce server-side processing requirements by transforming or filtering incoming data before storage.

Security remains a central concern in both agent-based and agentless monitoring. Agents should be configured to accept connections only from trusted Zabbix servers or proxies, use encrypted communication, and limit user parameter execution to known safe scripts. Agentless protocols such as SNMP and WMI should also be secured through access control lists, strong authentication, and encrypted channels when supported. Regular audits of monitoring configurations help ensure that unauthorized data exposure or system access is avoided.

In the long term, the choice between agent and agentless methods is not an either-or decision, but a question of selecting the right tool for the right context. As systems grow more diverse, from on-premises hardware to cloud-native microservices, Zabbix's flexible architecture and support for both methods ensures that administrators can continue to monitor reliably regardless of the underlying platform. Combining the depth of agent-based metrics with the reach of agentless protocols enables monitoring strategies that are both comprehensive and adaptable.

Chapter 8: Integrating Zabbix with External Tools and APIs

Integrating Zabbix with external tools and APIs significantly expands the functionality of the monitoring platform and enables seamless interaction with other systems, ranging from IT service management (ITSM) platforms and automation frameworks to communication tools and data visualization dashboards. Zabbix provides a comprehensive and well-documented API that supports RESTful operations over HTTP, allowing users to programmatically access nearly every function available in the Zabbix web interface. This includes creating and modifying hosts, templates, items, triggers, user accounts, actions, dashboards, and much more. The API uses JSON-RPC for request and response formatting, making it easy to integrate with various programming languages and automation tools such as Python, PowerShell, Bash, Ansible, and Terraform.

The most common use case for API integration is automating routine administrative tasks. For example, administrators can use the API to automatically register new hosts when systems are provisioned, apply appropriate templates based on host metadata, or update macros and trigger thresholds based on predefined conditions. In dynamic environments such as cloud platforms or container orchestration systems, where hosts are frequently created and destroyed, automation via the API ensures that Zabbix stays in sync with the actual infrastructure without requiring manual intervention.

When combined with orchestration tools like Ansible, a playbook can be written to deploy an application, install the Zabbix agent, and then call the Zabbix API to register the host, assign it to the correct host group, and link monitoring templates—all in a single, automated workflow.

The Zabbix API is also used for data extraction and integration with third-party reporting and analytics tools. Users can query historical data, event logs, problem statistics, and trend metrics to feed external dashboards, generate custom reports, or perform advanced analysis. For example, exporting Zabbix data into a business intelligence tool like Tableau or Power BI allows organizations to correlate infrastructure performance with business KPIs, track SLA compliance, or visualize trends over time. Developers can write scripts that authenticate with the Zabbix API, request specific item history using the history.get method, and then format the data for consumption by other systems.

Another important area of integration is with **ticketing and incident management systems**, where the goal is to streamline the process of turning alerts into actionable tickets. Zabbix can trigger notifications to platforms like Jira, ServiceNow, Zendesk, or Freshservice using **webhooks**, which are lightweight HTTP callbacks that send structured alert data in real time. Webhooks are configured as **media types** in Zabbix and can be customized using JavaScript-based transformation templates to ensure the payload matches the API schema of the target system. When a trigger fires, an action in Zabbix can invoke the webhook and automatically create a ticket, including details such as the affected host, problem description, severity, and timestamps. The integration can also support updates and closures, ensuring that ticket status changes reflect the problem state in Zabbix.

Zabbix's support for **webhook-based integrations** has grown substantially in recent versions, with a library of ready-to-use templates available for many popular platforms. These templates simplify the setup process and provide examples of how to format payloads, handle authentication, and manage error handling. For organizations that use chat platforms like Slack, Microsoft Teams, or Discord for incident response coordination, Zabbix can send alerts directly into channels with formatted messages, color-coded severity indicators, and embedded links to the Zabbix frontend for quick investigation. These integrations enhance team collaboration during incidents and ensure that alerts are delivered to the right people, in the right context, at the right time.

Beyond outbound integration, Zabbix can also receive data and commands from external systems through its **external scripts, user parameters**, and **web monitoring features**. External scripts allow Zabbix to execute custom scripts on the server or proxy side to perform checks that are not supported natively. These scripts can query APIs, run command-line tools, or evaluate complex conditions, returning results back into the Zabbix monitoring pipeline. For example, a script might call a cloud provider's API to check the status of virtual machines, or query a RESTful API to retrieve the health status of a microservice. User parameters work similarly but are configured on the agent side, enabling host-local data collection that goes beyond built-in item keys.

Web monitoring in Zabbix enables synthetic transaction monitoring, where the platform performs HTTP or HTTPS requests to a specified URL and evaluates the response based on status codes, content checks, and response times. This feature can be used to monitor the availability and performance of web applications, APIs, or services, and when combined with preprocessing and triggers, it provides a robust method of ensuring service health. In scenarios where external services need to push data into Zabbix, the **Zabbix sender** and **trapper items** can be used to accept input from custom scripts or monitoring agents. Zabbix sender is a command-line utility that can send values directly to the server, while trapper items allow Zabbix to passively receive values when triggered.

Integrations with **configuration management tools** such as Puppet, Chef, SaltStack, or Terraform are also possible through the API or custom scripting. These tools can be used to enforce consistent monitoring configurations across environments, ensure that every deployed system is correctly registered with Zabbix, and automatically remove decommissioned systems from the monitoring pool. By codifying monitoring logic as part of infrastructure-as-code practices, organizations can avoid configuration drift and maintain better control over the monitoring ecosystem.

For more advanced scenarios, Zabbix's API supports batching and bulk operations, reducing the overhead of multiple HTTP requests and improving performance in large-scale automation workflows. Authentication is handled via an API token or username-password combination, with sessions that can be reused across multiple calls. Fine-grained error messages help developers debug integration issues quickly, and extensive logging ensures traceability and auditability of all API actions.

Through these various integration capabilities—whether via API calls, webhooks, scripts, or external dashboards— Zabbix becomes more than a standalone monitoring tool. It transforms into a central hub for observability, operational awareness, and intelligent automation, tying together infrastructure telemetry with incident response, analytics, and decision-making processes. By connecting Zabbix with the broader ecosystem of IT and DevOps tools, organizations can eliminate silos, reduce response time, and gain comprehensive insight into the health and performance of their systems.

Chapter 9: Tuning Performance for Large Environments

Tuning performance for large environments in Zabbix requires a comprehensive understanding of the platform's internal architecture, data processing pipeline, and the way various components interact under load. As environments scale to hundreds or thousands of monitored hosts, each generating dozens or even hundreds of metrics per minute, the demand on CPU, memory, storage, and database performance increases significantly. Without proper tuning, performance bottlenecks can lead to delayed data collection, missed alerts, and increased response times across the user interface. The optimization process begins with an analysis of the Zabbix server's hardware and operating system environment. Ensuring that the server is provisioned with enough CPU cores, RAM, and fast disk I/O—preferably with SSD or NVMe storage—is fundamental. The server should also have a properly tuned kernel with optimized network stack parameters, particularly if a high volume of agent, SNMP, or trapper connections is expected.

The Zabbix server configuration file, typically located at /etc/zabbix/zabbix_server.conf, contains numerous parameters that directly impact performance. Among the most important are the process starters, such as StartPollers, StartTrappers, StartDBSyncers, StartDiscoverers, and StartPingers. Each of these parameters defines the number of parallel processes that Zabbix will spawn to handle specific types of tasks. In a large environment, the default values are often insufficient. For instance, if you are monitoring 10,000 hosts with 100,000 items, increasing StartPollers to 100 or more may be necessary to ensure that all checks are processed on time. Similar attention should be given to the number of trappers if you are receiving a large volume of passive data via trapper items or Zabbix sender.

Another critical setting is CacheSize, which determines how much memory is allocated for storing configuration data such as host definitions, item keys, triggers, and templates. If the cache size is too small, Zabbix will constantly reload configuration data from the database, leading to unnecessary I/O and CPU usage. The server log file will contain warnings like "Configuration cache is too small" if this value needs to be increased. Other cache-related settings include HistoryCacheSize, TrendCacheSize, ValueCacheSize, and HistoryIndexCacheSize. These control how much memory is dedicated to buffering historical values, trends, and indexing, and should be tuned according to the data volume and retention requirements.

Offloading data collection to Zabbix **proxies** is a recommended strategy for very large environments or geographically distributed networks. Proxies act as intermediaries, collecting and buffering data before sending it to the central server. This reduces the load on the main server, distributes polling activities, and improves fault tolerance by allowing data to be temporarily stored locally if the central server becomes unavailable. Proxies should also be configured with sufficient process starters and cache sizes based on the number of monitored hosts assigned to them. Using proxies helps isolate network segments, improve scalability, and avoid overwhelming the central server with data spikes.

The Zabbix **database** backend is another major performance consideration. Zabbix supports several databases, including MySQL, MariaDB, and PostgreSQL. Regardless of which one is used, the performance of the database directly affects the speed of data ingestion, dashboard responsiveness, and report generation. Tuning the database involves adjusting buffer pool sizes, query cache settings, connection limits, and write-ahead logging behavior. For MySQL or MariaDB, increasing the innodb_buffer_pool_size to 60–80% of total system memory ensures that most queries are served from memory rather than disk. Disabling the general query log and slow query log in production, unless actively troubleshooting, can reduce I/O overhead. PostgreSQL tuning may involve adjusting shared_buffers, work_mem, maintenance_work_mem, and effective_cache_size according to available system resources and workload characteristics.

Partitioning the Zabbix database tables is another advanced technique to improve performance, especially for large deployments where the history and trends tables grow rapidly. Partitioning splits large tables into smaller segments based on date or data type, allowing queries to access only relevant portions of the dataset. Although Zabbix does not support native partitioning out of the box, community-maintained scripts and cron jobs can automate the process. This reduces query times, speeds up data purging, and lowers the risk of table locks during maintenance operations.

Proper use of **preprocessing** can also improve performance by reducing the volume of raw data stored and processed. Preprocessing steps can include value transformations, regular expression extraction, data validation, throttling, or JSON/XML parsing. By cleaning and filtering the data before it is written to the database, Zabbix lowers the number of writes and helps focus on only meaningful values. Preprocessing is especially useful when working with log files, HTTP API responses, or SNMP traps that contain high-entropy or noisy data.

Reducing the frequency of low-priority checks is another best practice for performance tuning. While it might be tempting to monitor everything every 30 seconds, many metrics, such as disk usage, logged-in users, or service states, do not need such frequent updates. Adjusting the update interval of items to more sensible values—such as 300 seconds for rarely changing data—lowers the number of item checks per minute and reduces pressure on pollers and the database. Additionally, using **dependent items**, which derive their values from master items and are processed via preprocessing, can drastically cut down on polling operations.

The frontend user interface can also be a performance bottleneck if not optimized. Enabling server-side session compression, caching static assets, and using a reverse proxy like Nginx can reduce page load times and lighten the load on the web server. When dealing with very large dashboards or overviews, reducing the number of widgets or filtering the displayed data by host group or severity can lead to better responsiveness. Zabbix 5.x and above include performance improvements in the frontend, but thoughtful dashboard design and user access control remain important factors.

Housekeeping and data retention policies are also critical in maintaining long-term performance. Zabbix allows administrators to define how long historical data, trends, events, and audit logs should be stored. Keeping history data for 90 days and trend data for 365 days is a common balance, but in environments with compliance or audit requirements, these values might differ. Regularly purging outdated data reduces table sizes and speeds up queries. Automating database maintenance tasks such as index optimization and vacuuming also helps sustain performance over time.

Monitoring the monitoring system itself is essential. Zabbix provides internal checks for queue size, poller busy rates, cache usage, and database write performance. Watching these metrics helps identify when additional tuning is needed or when scaling the infrastructure further becomes necessary. By continuously analyzing and tuning the performance of the Zabbix server, database, proxies, and frontend, administrators ensure that the system remains responsive, reliable, and capable of supporting large and complex environments.

Chapter 10: Troubleshooting and Maintenance Essentials

Troubleshooting and maintenance are critical components of managing a Zabbix environment, ensuring that the monitoring system remains reliable, efficient, and capable of identifying issues before they affect production systems. As with any enterprise-grade platform, Zabbix may occasionally encounter configuration errors, performance bottlenecks, or unexpected behavior, and having a structured approach to diagnosing and resolving these issues helps maintain stability and trust in the monitoring infrastructure. One of the first steps in troubleshooting is to become familiar with the system logs, as they provide detailed insights into what the Zabbix server, proxy, and agent are doing at any given time. The primary Zabbix server log file, typically located at /var/log/zabbix/zabbix_server.log, records events related to database access, item processing, configuration loading, cache behavior, and internal process health. Reviewing this log for warnings or errors, especially those that occur repeatedly, is a valuable way to identify root causes early in the troubleshooting process.

Common log messages such as "Timeout while connecting to agent," "History cache is too small," or "Cannot send alert" each point to a different area requiring investigation, whether it's connectivity, memory allocation, or misconfigured media types. Increasing the debug level in the configuration file by setting DebugLevel=4 can reveal even more detail, though it should be used with caution in production environments due to the increased log verbosity. Zabbix proxies and agents have their own log files that are equally important when diagnosing issues in distributed or remote environments. For proxies, logs can help identify synchronization problems, network timeouts, or database writing failures. Agent logs are useful when items are not returning data as expected or if user parameters fail to execute.

In addition to checking logs, the Zabbix frontend provides several internal monitoring features that assist in identifying performance issues and operational problems. The **Zabbix queue**, accessible from the "Monitoring → Queue" section, shows how many items are delayed beyond their expected polling interval. A growing queue often indicates insufficient poller processes or overloaded proxies. Similarly, the **latest data** section allows users to verify whether items are collecting fresh data or remain outdated. If many items show "no data" or haven't updated in a long time, it might point to agent connectivity issues, firewall misconfigurations, or template misalignment. The **problems** view can also reveal misfiring triggers or repetitive alerts that may be caused by improperly tuned thresholds or noisy data sources.

Understanding Zabbix's internal metrics is crucial for proactive maintenance. These internal checks, available through a virtual host named "Zabbix server" or "Zabbix proxy," provide real-time feedback on poller load, cache usage, database performance, and queue lengths. Monitoring values such as zabbix[queue], zabbix[cache,history], and zabbix[trapper,values] can reveal whether adjustments are needed in the server configuration. For example, if cache usage consistently exceeds 80%, it is a sign that parameters like CacheSize or TrendCacheSize should be increased. Regularly checking the zabbix[process, ,busy] metrics helps determine if any internal processes are overburdened, such as pollers or trappers reaching maximum capacity, leading to slow data collection or alerting delays.

One frequent issue in larger environments is misconfigured item keys or template errors that prevent proper data collection. Verifying that each item is using a valid key supported by the agent or SNMP device helps reduce noise and focus attention on actionable data. In cases where custom user parameters are used, ensuring that the corresponding script exists, has correct permissions, and runs without error is essential. Executing these scripts manually on the target host can confirm whether the problem lies with the script or the Zabbix agent. It is also useful to validate agent connectivity using the zabbix_get command from the server or proxy, which simulates a data request and confirms that the agent is responsive and properly configured.

Routine maintenance tasks help avoid long-term degradation of performance and stability. One important task is regularly reviewing and cleaning up unused or obsolete items, triggers, and hosts. As infrastructure evolves, it is common for templates to become bloated or misaligned with the systems they are monitoring. Periodically auditing template contents and removing deprecated metrics ensures that only relevant data is being collected, reducing system load and database storage requirements. Similarly, removing hosts that are no longer in service prevents wasted resources and avoids confusion in dashboards and reports. When decommissioning hosts, it is advisable to disable them first, verify that no alerts or dependencies exist, and then remove them permanently.

Database maintenance is another essential part of keeping Zabbix healthy. Over time, history and trends tables can grow significantly, particularly in large environments with short update intervals. Ensuring that proper retention policies are in place and that the housekeeping process is functioning correctly helps prevent database bloat. Housekeeping is responsible for purging old data based on configured history and trend retention settings. If the process becomes too slow, it can be broken into multiple periods using the HousekeepingFrequency parameter or even offloaded to external scripts for partitioned databases. Database indexes should be monitored and optimized periodically, and tools like EXPLAIN for SQL queries can help identify slow operations that may affect the responsiveness of the frontend or data retrieval processes.

Regular backups of both the Zabbix database and configuration files are a best practice that ensures recovery from failures, human errors, or data corruption. The configuration files, including zabbix_server.conf, zabbix_agentd.conf, and proxy configurations, should be version-controlled and stored securely. Scheduled database dumps, along with testing the restoration process, ensure that disaster recovery procedures are in place and functional. Another valuable practice is maintaining a changelog of configuration modifications, such as new templates, macro updates, or trigger changes. This helps diagnose when a specific change might have introduced instability or unexpected behavior.

Keeping the Zabbix system up to date is also vital for long-term stability and security. Each new version introduces bug fixes, performance improvements, and new features that enhance the platform's capabilities. Before upgrading, it is important to review the release notes, back up the system, and test the upgrade process in a staging environment if possible. Following the correct upgrade sequence—proxy, server, and then frontend—ensures compatibility across components. After upgrading, reviewing logs and internal metrics helps verify that the system is operating as expected.

Monitoring the monitoring system itself is a concept that cannot be overstated. Setting up triggers and notifications on the availability of the Zabbix server, proxies, and agents ensures that any failure in the monitoring infrastructure is caught and addressed quickly. Alerting on internal checks like queue delays, high poller load, cache saturation, or failed database writes provides early warning signals of degradation. By combining regular maintenance with proactive monitoring and structured troubleshooting processes, administrators can ensure the continuous and reliable operation of Zabbix in any environment.

BOOK 2
SOLARWINDS UNLEASHED
ADVANCED IT INFRASTRUCTURE MANAGEMENT

ROB BOTWRIGHT

Chapter 1: SolarWinds Overview: Core Modules and Capabilities

SolarWinds is a comprehensive IT management platform known for its modular architecture and rich feature set designed to monitor, manage, and troubleshoot complex IT environments across networks, systems, applications, and cloud infrastructures. At the heart of the SolarWinds ecosystem lies the **Orion Platform**, a scalable and unified foundation that connects various monitoring modules into a single web-based interface. This integration allows administrators to monitor performance across different domains while maintaining a consistent user experience, centralized configuration, and unified alerting and reporting mechanisms. The modular nature of SolarWinds makes it flexible, allowing organizations to deploy only the components they need and expand as requirements grow.

One of the most widely used core modules is **Network Performance Monitor (NPM)**, which provides detailed visibility into the health and performance of network devices including routers, switches, firewalls, and wireless access points. NPM uses SNMP, ICMP, and other protocols to gather metrics such as latency, packet loss, interface utilization, CPU and memory usage, and device availability. It features dynamic network maps, NetPath visualization for path tracing, and advanced alerting that enables real-time detection of performance degradation or outages. The ability to create custom dashboards and drill down into device-specific statistics helps network engineers identify bottlenecks, misconfigurations, or failing hardware quickly.

Closely related to NPM is the **NetFlow Traffic Analyzer (NTA)**, which provides deep traffic flow analysis using NetFlow, J-Flow, sFlow, IPFIX, and other flow-based technologies. NTA helps administrators understand bandwidth consumption by identifying top talkers, protocols, applications, and conversations on the network. With its intuitive charts and traffic pattern analysis, NTA enables capacity planning, policy enforcement, and security anomaly detection by showing what is consuming network resources and whether traffic patterns align with expected usage. It integrates tightly with NPM to provide a holistic view of network performance and usage trends.

Server & Application Monitor (SAM) is another essential module that extends visibility beyond the network into servers and applications. SAM provides agentless and agent-based monitoring of Windows and Linux servers, virtual machines, and over 1,200 applications out of the box, including Microsoft Exchange, SQL Server, Active Directory, Apache, MySQL, and many others. It gathers performance metrics such as CPU load, memory usage, disk I/O, process availability, and application-specific counters. SAM includes AppInsight templates that provide in-depth visibility into complex services like SQL and IIS, giving administrators the tools to troubleshoot slow queries, failed logins, or configuration mismatches. Custom templates and scripts can be created for in-house or less common applications, allowing SAM to adapt to any environment.

Virtualization Manager (VMAN) offers specialized tools for monitoring virtual environments running on VMware or Hyper-V. VMAN provides real-time and historical performance data for virtual machines, hosts, clusters, and datastores. It identifies resource contention, wasted capacity, and misconfigured VMs, enabling administrators to optimize resource allocation and improve efficiency. VMAN also includes recommendations for rightsizing VMs, eliminating zombie VMs, and optimizing VM placement based on workload demands. It supports capacity planning through predictive analytics and integrates seamlessly with SAM and NPM to correlate virtual infrastructure health with application and network performance.

For managing storage infrastructures, **Storage Resource Monitor (SRM)** offers detailed visibility into multi-vendor SAN and NAS devices. SRM collects performance data such as read/write latency, throughput, disk usage, and IOPS from storage arrays by vendors like NetApp, EMC, Dell, HPE, and IBM. It provides end-to-end visibility into storage paths and helps identify underperforming volumes or hotspots affecting application performance. SRM's dashboards and reports support long-term planning, provisioning decisions, and troubleshooting storage-related issues in complex environments.

Database Performance Analyzer (DPA) is focused on optimizing SQL performance across multiple database platforms including Microsoft SQL Server, Oracle, MySQL, and PostgreSQL. DPA monitors query execution times, wait states, blocking sessions, and deadlocks to help database administrators pinpoint performance bottlenecks. Its anomaly detection engine highlights unusual behavior, and its historical data views assist with trend analysis and capacity planning. DPA can be used alongside SAM to provide a comprehensive picture of application stack health from the database layer to the end-user experience.

To ensure configuration compliance and streamline change tracking, SolarWinds offers **Network Configuration Manager (NCM)**, which automates the backup, comparison, and deployment of network device configurations. NCM supports policy compliance auditing against standards like PCI-DSS, HIPAA, or custom rules, and generates alerts when unauthorized or risky changes occur. Its integration with NPM provides context when a device's configuration change correlates with a performance issue, allowing faster root cause identification. NCM also supports mass configuration updates, firmware upgrades, and scheduled job automation across large device fleets.

SolarWinds includes robust **log management** capabilities through the **Log Analyzer** module, which ingests syslog, SNMP traps, and Windows event logs in real time. Logs can be filtered, searched, and correlated with performance metrics and alerts. This enables efficient root cause analysis by providing a full timeline of system behavior leading up to an issue. Log Analyzer integrates directly with the Orion console, making logs easily accessible during performance investigations.

User Device Tracker (UDT) enhances network security and visibility by identifying which users and devices are connected to specific switch ports or wireless access points. UDT provides historical connection data, helping administrators track rogue devices, enforce access policies, and maintain audit trails. It integrates with Active Directory and DHCP servers for enhanced context and supports alerting when unauthorized devices connect to the network.

IP Address Manager (IPAM) simplifies the management of IPv4 and IPv6 address spaces, DHCP scopes, and DNS entries.

It automates IP address allocation, detects IP conflicts, and provides subnet utilization reports. IPAM integrates with Microsoft, Cisco, and ISC DHCP/DNS servers to centralize address management, improve accuracy, and support audit compliance.

All these modules benefit from the centralized **Orion alerting engine**, which enables flexible and context-aware alerting across metrics, events, logs, and thresholds. Alerts can be triggered based on simple conditions or complex logical combinations and can initiate actions like sending emails, running scripts, creating tickets, or escalating incidents. The Orion **reporting system** allows scheduled or on-demand reports with customizable content, helping organizations meet operational and regulatory reporting needs.

The **Orion Platform API**, based on REST and SWIS (SolarWinds Information Service), allows external systems to interact with SolarWinds, automate tasks, extract data, or integrate with third-party tools. This level of extensibility makes SolarWinds a valuable component in larger IT automation and DevOps workflows.

Through its suite of tightly integrated modules and centralized management platform, SolarWinds provides a unified approach to monitoring the full IT stack—from network devices and servers to applications, databases, and storage—enabling operational excellence across hybrid and complex environments.

Chapter 2: Deploying the Orion Platform Step-by-Step

Deploying the Orion Platform step-by-step requires careful planning and execution to ensure a stable, scalable, and efficient monitoring environment that supports your organization's IT infrastructure needs. The deployment process begins with preparing the environment, which includes selecting appropriate hardware and software based on the size of the network, the number of monitored elements, and the performance expectations. SolarWinds provides sizing guidelines that help determine whether you should install all components on a single server or distribute them across multiple servers for larger environments. Key components include the Orion application server, the SQL database server, and optional additional polling engines and web servers, depending on the scale of the deployment.

The operating system for the Orion server should be a supported version of Microsoft Windows Server, typically 2016, 2019, or 2022, with the latest updates and service packs applied. Before installation, the server should be joined to the domain if required, have static IP settings configured, and meet minimum requirements for CPU, memory, and disk space. Installing the Orion Platform also requires a dedicated SQL Server instance, either on the same machine in smaller deployments or on a separate dedicated server for larger environments. Microsoft SQL Server Standard or Enterprise editions are recommended, and the database server should also be tuned for performance with considerations like setting the appropriate maximum memory usage, enabling TCP/IP protocols, and ensuring proper disk I/O throughput.

Once the hardware and OS prerequisites are in place, the next step is to download the SolarWinds Orion Installer from the Customer Portal or SolarWinds website. This unified installer streamlines the process of deploying the core platform and selected modules like Network Performance Monitor (NPM), Server & Application Monitor (SAM), or NetFlow Traffic Analyzer (NTA). Running the installer as a local administrator launches the setup wizard, which guides users through module selection, prerequisite checks, and installation location. The installer automatically installs required Windows features such as IIS (Internet Information Services), .NET Framework, and MSMQ if they are not already present.

During the installation process, the wizard prompts for the SQL Server database connection details. You can specify an existing database instance or allow the installer to create a new database for Orion. Windows Authentication or SQL Authentication can be used, but the selected account must have sufficient privileges to create and configure the Orion database. After database configuration, the installer sets up the necessary services, application files, and the Orion Web Console. This process can take several minutes to complete, depending on the selected modules and system performance.

Once the installation is complete, the Configuration Wizard automatically launches. This tool finalizes the setup by configuring the database schema, registering services, and initializing web components. It also checks for updates and verifies communication between all Orion services. During this step, administrators can also specify the credentials used for polling devices and collecting metrics, such as SNMP community strings, WMI access credentials, or agent-based polling settings.

After the Configuration Wizard completes successfully, the Orion Web Console becomes available, typically accessed by navigating to http://<hostname or IP address>/orion from a supported web browser. The first-time login uses the default admin account, and you are prompted to change the password and configure initial settings such as time zone, SMTP server details for alerting, and default polling intervals. The Web Console provides a centralized interface for managing all aspects of the Orion Platform, including node discovery, alert configuration, dashboard customization, and report generation.

The next critical step is discovering network devices and systems to monitor. The Orion Platform includes a powerful network discovery engine that can scan subnets, import devices from spreadsheets, or integrate with Active Directory. During the discovery process, administrators can define SNMP versions, WMI credentials, and preferred polling methods. Discovered devices are listed with associated metadata, and you can choose which elements to import into monitoring. Devices can be grouped by role, location, or department using custom properties and dynamic groups, helping to organize the environment for easier management.

Once devices are added, the Orion Platform begins polling metrics such as CPU load, memory usage, disk space, interface status, and response time. Monitoring templates and component monitors can be applied to servers and applications to collect deeper insights, especially when modules like SAM or VMAN are installed. Administrators can fine-tune polling intervals, thresholds, and alerting rules based on the organization's needs. Alert actions can include email notifications, SMS messages, syslog generation, SNMP traps, or integration with external systems like ServiceNow, Jira, or Microsoft Teams.

Dashboards and views can now be customized to reflect different roles or focus areas. The Orion Web Console allows the creation of summary views, top talkers, network maps, and real-time charts, each tailored to specific teams such as network operations, server administrators, or helpdesk staff. Custom properties can be used as filters and grouping mechanisms, making it easier to segment large environments. Additional web servers can be deployed to distribute user access load, especially in environments with many concurrent users or geographically dispersed teams.

Optional polling engines can be deployed to increase scalability by distributing polling tasks across multiple systems. This is particularly important in large environments or when polling frequencies are high. The Additional Polling Engine (APE) installation is performed using the same installer and connects to the same Orion database. After deployment, polling loads can be balanced between engines to ensure optimal performance and minimal latency.

For long-term success, administrators should also implement regular maintenance tasks, including backups of the Orion database, performance tuning for SQL Server, and review of system logs and alerts. The Orion Platform includes diagnostic tools such as the SolarWinds Diagnostic Tool and Performance Analyzer, which help identify issues with polling performance, database queries, or web console responsiveness. Keeping the system updated with the latest hotfixes and patches is essential, and SolarWinds provides regular software updates that address security, stability, and feature enhancements.

Security best practices during deployment include enforcing HTTPS for web access, using strong service account credentials, limiting SNMP access to trusted IP ranges, and regularly reviewing user roles and permissions within the Orion Web Console. Role-based access control ensures that users only see and interact with the resources relevant to their responsibilities. Two-factor authentication, IP restrictions, and logging of user activity are additional layers that strengthen the deployment from a security standpoint.

By following a structured, step-by-step approach, the deployment of the Orion Platform provides a solid foundation for unified IT monitoring across diverse and complex environments. This approach ensures a stable installation, optimized performance, and a scalable framework that supports both current and future monitoring needs.

Chapter 3: Network Performance Monitor (NPM) in Depth

Network Performance Monitor (NPM) is one of the cornerstone modules within the SolarWinds Orion Platform, designed to provide comprehensive visibility into the performance, availability, and health of network devices across an organization's infrastructure. It enables IT professionals to monitor a wide range of devices such as routers, switches, firewalls, load balancers, wireless controllers, and access points, regardless of vendor, through the use of standard protocols like SNMP, ICMP, and CLI. NPM offers real-time and historical data collection, advanced alerting, intelligent visualizations, and powerful diagnostic tools that together allow teams to detect, diagnose, and resolve network issues before they impact users or critical business operations.

The deployment of NPM begins with device discovery, which is the process of scanning the network to identify devices and interfaces that can be monitored. The discovery engine supports IP range scanning, subnet scanning, and Active Directory-based discovery, making it easy to onboard new devices into the monitoring system. During discovery, SNMP credentials are used to query devices and collect essential information such as device type, vendor, model, serial number, firmware version, and the list of interfaces. Once discovered, devices can be grouped logically by department, location, or function using custom properties, and these groupings can be used to create views, filters, and alert scopes.

Once devices are imported into NPM, polling begins immediately using default or customized polling intervals. Polling includes metrics such as interface traffic (in and out), interface status (up/down), CPU usage, memory consumption, error and discard rates, temperature, fan speed, and power supply status. For WAN and internet links, NPM provides jitter, latency, and packet loss monitoring, giving deep insight into the quality of service across connections. One of the key features of NPM is its ability to present this data in a user-friendly and actionable way through dashboards, charts, and performance views.

NetPath is a diagnostic feature within NPM that visualizes the path packets take from a source to a destination, including internal and external hops. Unlike traditional traceroute, NetPath provides graphical path views, latency per hop, and real-time status, allowing administrators to pinpoint exactly where delays or failures occur along a network path. This is particularly useful when troubleshooting cloud-based application performance, as it reveals where third-party networks may be introducing delays. NetPath's continuous monitoring helps identify intermittent issues that are difficult to catch with manual tools.

NPM also includes network topology mapping, which automatically builds visual maps of device interconnections based on Layer 2 and Layer 3 relationships. These maps can be customized and embedded into dashboards for operational visibility. Dynamic updates to the maps occur as devices are added or removed, ensuring the visualizations reflect the current state of the network. Layer 2 topology detection leverages information from CDP, LLDP, and bridge MIBs to determine switch port connections and visualize access-layer relationships, while Layer 3 discovery maps routing paths and connections between core devices.

Wireless network monitoring is another core capability within NPM. It supports visibility into wireless LAN controllers, access points, and connected clients, offering metrics such as signal strength, channel utilization, client count per SSID, and roaming behavior. Administrators can monitor controller load, detect access point failures, and track client connectivity issues in real time. Historical wireless usage data can help optimize coverage, balance client loads, and identify rogue devices or unauthorized access.

Another advanced feature in NPM is the concept of interface monitoring profiles and thresholds. Administrators can define critical, warning, and informational thresholds for metrics such as bandwidth utilization, errors, and discards. These thresholds can be applied globally or overridden per interface or device, providing flexibility in how alerts are triggered. The alerting engine in NPM is highly customizable, allowing multi-condition alerts, suppression rules, escalation policies, and integration with notification systems such as email, SMS, Slack, or ticketing platforms like ServiceNow or Jira. Alerts can include rich contextual information such as affected device, last known status, related events, and recommended actions.

NPM also provides powerful reporting tools that allow users to schedule and generate performance and availability reports. Reports can include interface statistics, uptime summaries, alert history, device inventory, and custom KPIs. The report scheduler supports PDF, CSV, and web-based delivery, enabling stakeholders to receive relevant updates automatically. Custom reports can be built using the web-based Report Writer or directly from SQL queries for advanced use cases.

Performance analysis in NPM is enhanced by the PerfStack tool, which provides drag-and-drop performance correlation across time. Users can select multiple devices, metrics, and time ranges, and visualize them on a single timeline chart. This helps in identifying correlated spikes, bottlenecks, and cause-effect relationships between different parts of the network. For example, if a web server is experiencing slow response times, PerfStack can be used to correlate server performance, interface utilization, and latency to see if the root cause lies in the network layer.

The customizable dashboards in NPM allow users to create role-specific views tailored to network operations, executive management, or helpdesk teams. Dashboards can include widgets such as top talkers, node availability charts, traffic trend graphs, event summaries, and custom maps. Interactive elements allow users to drill down from summary views into detailed metrics for troubleshooting and analysis. Network health scores and SLA dashboards provide quick indicators of network performance against defined thresholds or service level objectives.

NPM also supports high availability (HA) configurations, ensuring that monitoring continues even if the primary Orion server fails. In HA setups, a standby server takes over without data loss or service interruption, preserving critical alerting and monitoring functionality. NPM's scalability is further enhanced by adding polling engines and web servers to distribute processing and support more users and devices.

Security is addressed through role-based access control, audit trails, and encryption of sensitive data such as SNMP credentials. User roles define who can view, modify, or administer different aspects of the system, allowing organizations to implement least-privilege principles. NPM supports integration with Active Directory for authentication and can log user activity for compliance and auditing.

With its deep visibility into device health, interface performance, wireless networks, path analysis, and historical trends, NPM serves as the central tool for network monitoring and troubleshooting in many enterprise environments. It helps reduce mean time to resolution (MTTR), improve service uptime, and provide actionable insights to support business continuity. Through intuitive visualizations, intelligent alerts, and seamless integration with other Orion modules, Network Performance Monitor empowers IT teams to manage network complexity with confidence and precision.

Chapter 4: Setting Up Alerts, Reports, and Automation

Setting up alerts, reports, and automation in the SolarWinds Orion Platform is a critical step in transforming raw monitoring data into actionable intelligence that helps IT teams maintain uptime, optimize performance, and respond to incidents in a timely and consistent manner. The Orion Platform provides a robust and flexible alerting engine that supports both simple and complex conditions, enabling administrators to create precise notification policies tailored to their environment and operational workflows. Alert configurations can be based on virtually any monitored metric, including network latency, bandwidth utilization, CPU and memory usage, application status, response time, or even log messages and custom metrics gathered via scripts or APIs.

The process of setting up an alert begins with defining the **trigger conditions**, which are the specific thresholds or patterns that must be met for the alert to be activated. These conditions can include numeric comparisons, such as "CPU usage greater than 90% for more than 5 minutes," or logical combinations of multiple factors, such as "interface status is down AND packet loss exceeds 20%." Administrators can also include time-based logic, such as triggering alerts only during business hours, or using sliding windows to detect sustained issues instead of brief spikes. The alert system allows for dynamic variables and custom properties, making it possible to reuse alert definitions across different nodes, interfaces, or groups while maintaining relevant context.

Once the trigger conditions are defined, the next step is to configure the **alert actions**, which define what should happen when the alert is fired. Common actions include sending an email or SMS to designated recipients, generating a syslog message, writing to the Windows Event Log, creating an SNMP trap, or executing a script or external program. More advanced integrations can include sending notifications via webhooks to platforms like Slack, Microsoft Teams, ServiceNow, or Jira. These actions can be sequenced, scheduled with delays, and combined with escalation rules to ensure that unresolved issues are brought to the attention of the right personnel as quickly as possible.

The alerting engine also supports **reset conditions**, which define when an alert should be considered resolved and notifications should be stopped. For example, if an alert is triggered when disk space drops below 10%, the reset condition might be set to clear the alert when disk space returns above 15%, avoiding alert flapping caused by minor metric fluctuations. In addition, alerts can be configured with **acknowledgment requirements**, allowing administrators or support staff to manually confirm that they are aware of the issue. This acknowledgment can be used to suppress further notifications, track incident response, and support compliance with incident management procedures.

SolarWinds also includes **alert suppression** features to prevent unnecessary alerts during planned maintenance windows, known downtimes, or cascading failures. For example, if a core router becomes unreachable, alerts for all downstream devices can be automatically suppressed, reducing alert noise and helping operators focus on the root cause. Suppression can be configured through dependency relationships, custom properties, or manual control from the web interface. Alert history and notification logs are stored in the Orion database, providing a detailed audit trail of when alerts occurred, who received them, and how they were handled.

In parallel with alerting, the Orion Platform provides extensive **reporting capabilities**, allowing administrators to generate periodic summaries of network, system, or application health. Reports can include data such as availability percentages, top bandwidth consumers, peak CPU usage, compliance with service level agreements, or custom metrics defined by the organization. The web-based **Report Writer** allows users to create reports using a graphical interface, selecting data sources, filtering by node or time range, and applying custom formatting. Reports can be generated on demand or scheduled for automatic delivery via email to stakeholders, managers, or auditors.

Reports support multiple output formats, including HTML, PDF, and CSV, and can be embedded in dashboards or exported for further analysis in external tools like Excel or Power BI. Templates are available for common reporting needs, and custom SQL-based reports can be created for advanced use cases. Administrators can control report visibility through role-based access permissions, ensuring that users only see reports relevant to their responsibilities. The scheduling engine allows reports to be generated hourly, daily, weekly, or monthly, supporting both operational monitoring and long-term trend analysis.

Automation in the Orion Platform goes beyond alerts and reports, extending into **automated remediation and orchestration**. Through the use of alert actions that execute scripts or external programs, the system can automatically respond to certain conditions without human intervention. For instance, if a service stops on a monitored server, an alert can trigger a PowerShell or Bash script to restart the service automatically. If a firewall rule changes unexpectedly, a script can revert the configuration or notify security staff. These automation routines help reduce mean time to resolution and prevent minor issues from escalating into major outages.

Another layer of automation comes through **Orion SDK** and **SolarWinds API**, which allow administrators to script interactions with the platform using tools like PowerShell, Python, or RESTful HTTP calls. Using the API, teams can automate the creation and removal of nodes, update monitoring settings, change alert configurations, or extract monitoring data for use in other systems. Combined with configuration management tools like Ansible, Chef, or Puppet, the API allows full integration of SolarWinds monitoring into infrastructure-as-code pipelines and CI/CD workflows, supporting agile and DevOps environments.

Automation is also supported through dynamic object groups and **custom properties**, which can be used to drive behavior based on context. For example, nodes tagged with "critical" can be monitored more aggressively or escalated faster in alerting policies. Devices can be grouped dynamically by location, operating system, department, or any other tag, and these groups can be used as filters in alert conditions, report generation, or dashboard views. This dynamic behavior reduces the need for manual updates and ensures that changes in infrastructure are automatically reflected in the monitoring configuration.

By combining intelligent alerts, automated reports, and customizable automation routines, the Orion Platform empowers IT teams to be more proactive, responsive, and efficient in maintaining system health and ensuring continuous service delivery. These capabilities transform raw monitoring data into practical insights and repeatable actions that align with business goals and reduce the burden on technical staff.

Chapter 5: Customizing Dashboards and Views

Customizing dashboards and views in the SolarWinds Orion Platform is a powerful way to tailor the monitoring experience to meet the specific needs of different users, teams, and departments within an organization. The Orion Web Console provides a highly flexible interface that allows administrators to create personalized views containing exactly the data, charts, alerts, and visual elements relevant to the role of each user. Custom dashboards reduce information overload, help focus attention on what matters most, and improve response time by bringing critical insights to the forefront. The customization process begins with understanding the available **view types**, which include summary views, node details, interface views, application views, and custom views. Each of these can be modified or entirely recreated to display data in a layout and format that makes sense for the end user.

Dashboards are composed of **widgets**, which are modular elements that present data in specific formats such as graphs, tables, gauges, maps, text boxes, or dynamic lists. Each widget is configurable and can be filtered based on object properties, time ranges, or severity levels. Common widgets include Top 10 lists, alert lists, traffic charts, custom HTML content, network maps, and PerfStack performance views. Widgets can be resized and arranged freely on the page, enabling users to prioritize visual content based on importance. For example, a NOC team might want a large real-time alert feed and map of device statuses at the top of their dashboard, while a server team may focus on system load graphs and disk space summaries.

Custom dashboards can be created for individual users, user groups, or globally shared to ensure consistency across the organization. Role-based access control ensures that users only see the data they are authorized to access, which is especially important in multi-team or multi-tenant environments. This allows a network engineer to view and interact with switches and routers while an application team member sees only web server and database metrics. By controlling visibility at the view and widget level, administrators can ensure compliance with data access policies and improve usability by eliminating irrelevant data.

The process of building a custom dashboard starts with selecting a view to clone or starting from a blank template. The administrator chooses a column layout, such as one-column, two-column, or a flexible multi-column layout. Widgets are then added from a list of available types. Each widget is configured through a dialog box where the data source, filters, and display parameters are defined. For example, when configuring a "Top 10 Interfaces by Traffic" widget, the user can define the interface type, polling interval, time range, and whether to sort by inbound or outbound traffic. If a custom property like "Location" or "ServiceTier" is assigned to nodes, it can also be used to filter the data shown in the widget.

Maps can be embedded directly into dashboards to provide a real-time geographical or logical view of the network. These maps can show node and interface statuses using color-coded icons and can include interactive elements such as links to node details or tooltips showing the most recent performance data. Maps update automatically based on the underlying device statuses, making them highly useful in operational centers. Similarly, graphs and charts can be embedded to show historical trends, allowing users to visualize performance over time. This helps in identifying patterns, anomalies, or degradation that may not trigger alerts but indicate long-term issues.

Orion supports **custom HTML widgets**, allowing administrators to embed external content, display formatted text, or include links to third-party tools. These widgets support JavaScript and CSS, enabling deeper integration with existing dashboards or branding them to match corporate identity. This capability is particularly useful for teams that want to integrate business KPIs, service status pages, or external reporting tools into a unified console experience. HTML widgets can also be used for operational notes, instructions, or contact information to support team coordination.

Another feature that enhances dashboard customization is the use of **dynamic queries and custom properties**, which allow dashboards to adapt automatically to infrastructure changes. For instance, a dashboard configured to display all critical nodes in a specific data center can update in real time as nodes are added or removed from that location. By tagging devices with custom properties such as "BusinessUnit," "Priority," or "Environment," and then using those tags as filters in widgets, administrators can build dashboards that organize data in a meaningful, business-relevant structure. This also allows for dashboards to remain relevant even in fast-changing environments such as cloud-native deployments or DevOps-driven pipelines.

Views can also be tied to user accounts, allowing administrators to assign default home pages and starting views for different roles. For example, a helpdesk technician might log in to a simplified dashboard showing only open tickets, active alerts, and a list of user-facing systems, while a network architect sees a topology map, bandwidth usage, and router CPU statistics. This ensures that each user begins their session with information that is immediately useful, without needing to dig through unrelated data.

In large environments, managing a growing number of dashboards and views can be streamlined through the use of **view folders** and naming conventions. Administrators can group dashboards by function, team, or project, ensuring that users can easily find the view they need. Scheduled dashboard rotations can also be configured for large display screens in control rooms, cycling through multiple views at set intervals to provide continuous visibility into different parts of the infrastructure.

The Orion Web Console also allows cloning and exporting of dashboards, which is useful for replicating successful layouts across teams or environments. Exported views can be stored in version control systems or included in documentation, supporting change management and rollback procedures. When used in combination with automation tools or the SolarWinds API, dashboard configurations can be deployed programmatically, enabling infrastructure-as-code practices for monitoring environments.

Customizing dashboards and views in the Orion Platform transforms the monitoring experience from a static list of metrics into a dynamic, interactive, and user-centered interface that adapts to the needs of the business. By leveraging the wide array of widgets, dynamic filtering, custom properties, and visual elements available, teams can build dashboards that not only display data but tell a story about the health, performance, and reliability of their systems. Through thoughtful design and continuous refinement, dashboards become essential tools for proactive monitoring, incident response, and strategic decision-making across the entire IT landscape.

Chapter 6: Monitoring Servers, Applications, and Cloud Services

Monitoring servers, applications, and cloud services is a core capability of the SolarWinds Orion Platform, enabling IT teams to gain visibility across on-premises infrastructure, hosted applications, and hybrid environments. With the increasing complexity of modern IT operations, having a unified view of system health, application performance, and service availability is critical for maintaining uptime, delivering consistent user experiences, and resolving issues before they escalate into major incidents. SolarWinds Server & Application Monitor (SAM) is the primary module responsible for this layer of observability, and it integrates tightly with other Orion modules such as Network Performance Monitor (NPM), Virtualization Manager (VMAN), and NetFlow Traffic Analyzer (NTA) to provide correlated insights across the full stack.

Monitoring begins with **server visibility**, where SAM collects a wide range of performance metrics from Windows and Linux systems using agentless or agent-based methods. These metrics include CPU usage, memory utilization, disk I/O, network traffic, service availability, and process status. For Windows systems, SAM uses WMI or SNMP to poll metrics, while for Linux systems, it typically relies on SSH-based polling or SNMP. In environments where agents are preferred, SolarWinds supports lightweight agents that offer more frequent polling intervals, reduced load on polling engines, and better scalability for large distributed deployments. Server monitoring includes not only resource usage but also the state of services, scheduled tasks, user sessions, and system events.

The next layer focuses on **application monitoring**, which is where SAM truly excels by offering over 1,200 out-of-the-box application templates covering a wide range of enterprise applications and services. These include Microsoft applications such as Exchange, SQL Server, Active Directory, IIS, and SharePoint, as well as open-source and cross-platform technologies like Apache, MySQL, PostgreSQL, Tomcat, and Nginx. Each template contains predefined component monitors tailored to the application being monitored, collecting performance counters, log file entries, configuration values, and service statuses. Component monitors can include scripts, Windows performance counters, SNMP OIDs, WMI queries, and log matchers, offering flexibility to adapt to custom or in-house applications.

SAM's **AppInsight** feature provides deep, application-aware monitoring for complex platforms like SQL Server and IIS. AppInsight for SQL Server, for example, tracks query execution times, transaction log sizes, buffer cache hit ratios, deadlocks, index fragmentation, and other advanced database metrics. This granularity allows database administrators to troubleshoot performance issues such as slow queries or blocking sessions directly from the Orion Web Console, without needing to jump into SSMS or external tools. AppInsight for IIS offers detailed metrics around worker processes, site response times, HTTP error codes, and request queues, helping teams quickly identify application bottlenecks at the web server level.

Cloud service monitoring is another area where SolarWinds has expanded its capabilities to support the shift toward hybrid and multi-cloud architectures. With SAM and additional plugins or integrations, administrators can monitor services from public cloud providers such as Amazon Web Services (AWS), Microsoft Azure, and Google Cloud Platform (GCP). This includes visibility into virtual machines, cloud-native services like AWS RDS or Azure App Services, storage usage, CPU credits, and service availability. Cloud metrics can be collected using APIs or agent-based polling, depending on the deployment model and level of detail required. SolarWinds offers templates specifically designed to connect to cloud APIs, retrieve usage and performance data, and integrate that data into existing dashboards, alerts, and reports.

Another important capability is **hardware health monitoring**, where SAM uses protocols like IPMI, SNMP, and WMI to track physical parameters such as fan speeds, power supply status, system temperatures, and RAID health on supported hardware from vendors like Dell, HP, Lenovo, and Cisco. These hardware health metrics are critical for identifying failures or degradation at the physical layer, especially in data centers or branch offices where remote hands-on diagnostics may not be immediately available.

Monitoring is further enhanced through **custom templates**, which allow administrators to create their own monitoring definitions for proprietary or non-standard applications. These templates can include custom scripts, command outputs, registry values, REST API responses, or database queries, and they support logic for determining thresholds, expected output, and error conditions. Templates can be reused across multiple nodes, allowing consistency in monitoring and simplifying maintenance. When combined with custom properties and dynamic groups, these templates become even more powerful, automatically applying the correct monitors as new servers or services are added.

Dashboards and performance views offer real-time insights into monitored servers and applications. Users can create summary views for server health, application status, response times, or alert volumes. Dashboards can include widgets such as CPU load graphs, application availability charts, top resource consumers, and service maps showing dependencies between infrastructure and applications. These views can be tailored to different teams such as database admins, web developers, or cloud architects, ensuring that each group sees the data most relevant to their responsibilities.

Alerting is integrated deeply with application and server monitoring, allowing teams to define specific thresholds for warning and critical states. For example, if an application pool stops, CPU usage exceeds 95% for five minutes, or a specific log message is detected, SAM can generate an alert and take automated action. Actions might include sending a notification, opening a ticket in an ITSM platform, restarting a service, or executing a remediation script. These alert conditions can be tuned to match business hours, maintenance windows, or server roles, ensuring that alerts are meaningful and actionable.

Historical reporting and trend analysis support capacity planning, SLA compliance, and executive reporting. SAM allows users to generate scheduled or ad hoc reports showing application uptime, resource consumption, alert frequencies, and performance baselines. Reports can be filtered by node, application, time range, or custom property, and exported in various formats such as PDF or CSV. These reports help teams plan for infrastructure upgrades, demonstrate compliance with internal or external standards, and support root cause analysis after incidents.

Virtualization monitoring is seamlessly integrated with SAM when combined with VMAN. This allows visibility into host and guest performance, VM sprawl, datastore usage, and hypervisor health. The integration helps correlate application performance with underlying virtualization infrastructure, allowing teams to determine whether a slow application is caused by a VM-level issue, such as resource contention, or an issue within the application stack itself.

Through its rich set of tools for monitoring servers, applications, and cloud services, the SolarWinds Orion Platform enables a unified, correlated view of IT operations. Whether tracking CPU spikes on a Linux server, monitoring the availability of an internal web app, or observing the performance of a cloud database, the platform provides the flexibility, scalability, and intelligence needed to ensure high availability, rapid incident resolution, and optimal service delivery across a complex and evolving infrastructure landscape.

Chapter 7: Managing Network Configuration and Compliance

Managing network configuration and compliance is a vital responsibility for IT teams, especially in complex and regulated environments where even small misconfigurations can lead to security vulnerabilities, performance degradation, or service outages. Within the SolarWinds Orion Platform, this task is primarily handled by the **Network Configuration Manager (NCM)** module, which provides a comprehensive set of tools to automate configuration backup, track changes, enforce compliance, and streamline auditing processes across a wide variety of network devices. NCM supports switches, routers, firewalls, wireless controllers, and other network appliances from vendors such as Cisco, Juniper, Palo Alto, HP, Arista, and many others, using standard protocols like SSH and Telnet to connect and interact with device command-line interfaces.

The first step in managing network configuration with NCM is to establish secure connectivity to all relevant network devices. This involves specifying device credentials, connection methods, and access policies. NCM supports both individual login credentials and shared credential sets, allowing administrators to efficiently manage access to hundreds or thousands of devices without duplicating configuration. Once access is configured, NCM can be scheduled to perform **nightly or periodic backups** of running and startup configurations, ensuring that the current state of every device is securely archived and available for comparison or restoration. These backups are stored in the NCM database and can be encrypted for security, providing a historical record of every configuration version across the environment.

Automated backups serve multiple purposes, including disaster recovery and troubleshooting. If a device fails or a change leads to unexpected behavior, administrators can quickly restore the last known good configuration from NCM's archive. Configuration versions are time-stamped and tagged with metadata, making it easy to identify when a change was made and by whom. NCM can also perform **configuration diffing**, visually highlighting the differences between any two versions of a configuration file. This feature is useful for understanding what changed during a maintenance window, whether a new policy was correctly applied, or if unauthorized changes occurred outside of approved procedures.

Change tracking and alerting are tightly integrated into NCM's workflow. When a new configuration is detected, NCM can trigger an alert, generate a syslog message, or create an email notification to inform network administrators. This real-time visibility helps reduce the time between a change occurring and it being noticed, which is especially valuable in environments where network stability and uptime are mission-critical. Change detection can be based on complete configuration files or filtered sections, allowing fine-grained control over what constitutes a significant modification. For example, changes to an access control list or routing table may be considered high-priority, while interface description updates may be ignored.

NCM also supports **configuration standardization** through the use of configuration templates and snippets. These can be used to define standardized settings for interface configurations, SNMP community strings, logging policies, and security rules. Administrators can apply these templates across multiple devices or groups, ensuring consistency and reducing the risk of errors caused by manual configuration. Bulk configuration changes can be pushed from NCM to devices using scripts or command sequences, and these changes can be scheduled, tested, and documented for compliance purposes. This functionality is particularly useful during firmware upgrades, policy rollouts, or network expansion projects, where consistency across devices is essential.

Compliance auditing is another core feature of NCM, supporting both internal policy enforcement and external regulatory requirements. NCM includes a built-in compliance engine that allows administrators to define rules and policies that devices must meet. These rules can include checks for password complexity, SSH-only access, disabled unused services, logging configurations, and adherence to specific command sequences. NCM can automatically scan device configurations against these rules and generate compliance reports showing which devices pass or fail, along with detailed explanations of the violations. This helps organizations maintain alignment with frameworks such as PCI-DSS, HIPAA, SOX, NIST, and ISO 27001.

Custom compliance policies can be created using regular expressions and rule logic, allowing organizations to enforce their own standards or adapt existing frameworks to suit their specific environment. Rules can be grouped into policies and assigned to device groups, making it easy to segment compliance requirements by function, location, or risk level. The results of compliance scans are presented in dashboards and reports that include summary scores, detailed violations, and historical trends, providing visibility for both operational teams and auditors. Automated remediation can also be configured, allowing NCM to correct non-compliant configurations by applying predefined fixes or reverting unauthorized changes.

To enhance security, NCM includes **role-based access control (RBAC)**, ensuring that only authorized users can make changes, access sensitive configuration files, or run compliance scans. Activities are logged and tracked for accountability, and audit trails can be exported for review. NCM can be integrated with Active Directory to simplify user management and enforce group-based permissions. Multi-user environments benefit from approval workflows, where proposed configuration changes can be reviewed and approved before deployment, reducing the likelihood of unintentional disruptions.

Integration with other Orion modules adds further value to NCM by correlating configuration changes with performance or availability issues. For example, if a router's CPU usage spikes or a service becomes unreachable shortly after a configuration change, administrators can use PerfStack or NetPath to identify the issue and NCM to trace the root cause. This cross-functional visibility accelerates troubleshooting and supports better incident response. NCM's integration with the Orion alert engine also means that compliance violations or failed configuration backups can trigger alerts, opening tickets in ITSM systems or notifying responsible teams automatically.

Scheduled reports in NCM provide stakeholders with up-to-date information on configuration status, compliance levels, and change history. Reports can be delivered via email, exported as PDFs, or accessed through the web interface, supporting daily operational oversight and long-term auditing needs. These reports can include charts, trend lines, and device summaries, helping IT leaders identify patterns, plan remediation efforts, and demonstrate compliance during audits.

In large, distributed environments, managing configurations manually becomes increasingly difficult and prone to error. NCM's ability to automate backup, track every change, enforce compliance, and standardize configurations across vendors and locations significantly reduces operational risk. Whether responding to security audits, preparing for compliance checks, or recovering from misconfigurations, the tools provided by SolarWinds Network Configuration Manager empower teams to maintain control, consistency, and confidence in their network infrastructure.

Chapter 8: Integrating SolarWinds with External Systems

Integrating SolarWinds with external systems is essential for creating a cohesive IT operations ecosystem that connects monitoring data with incident management, automation, reporting, and collaboration tools. The SolarWinds Orion Platform provides multiple integration points including APIs, webhooks, and external script execution, enabling organizations to extend the value of their monitoring data across various departments, workflows, and technologies. The primary interface for integration is the **SolarWinds Orion SDK**, which includes a RESTful API and the SolarWinds Information Service (SWIS). These interfaces allow programmatic access to the Orion database, enabling read and write operations such as retrieving metrics, updating nodes, creating alerts, or automating device management.

The **Orion API** supports REST and SOAP protocols and returns data in JSON or XML format, making it accessible through programming languages like Python, PowerShell, JavaScript, and C#. Common integration use cases include automating device onboarding, updating custom properties, retrieving performance data, or syncing Orion configuration with CMDB systems. For example, when a new server is provisioned through an infrastructure-as-code tool like Terraform, an accompanying API call to SolarWinds can automatically register the new node, assign it to the correct group, apply monitoring templates, and configure alerting policies. This reduces manual effort and ensures that newly deployed resources are monitored from the moment they come online.

Integrating SolarWinds with **IT service management (ITSM)** platforms such as ServiceNow, Jira Service Management, or BMC Remedy enables seamless incident creation, update, and closure workflows based on alerts generated in the Orion Platform. Through the use of **webhooks**, SolarWinds can send structured HTTP POST requests to external URLs when predefined alert conditions are met. These requests contain dynamic content such as the node name, IP address, alert message, severity, and timestamp, which can be used by the receiving platform to create detailed incident tickets. This allows alerting to be tightly coupled with ticketing and response processes, ensuring that issues are tracked, assigned, and resolved according to defined SLAs. Webhooks can also be used to send alerts to collaboration tools like Slack or Microsoft Teams, providing real-time visibility for support teams within their daily communication platforms.

In addition to webhooks and APIs, **external scripts** can be executed as part of alert actions or scheduled tasks. These scripts may be written in PowerShell, Bash, Python, or other languages supported by the environment and can be used to trigger remediation tasks, collect additional diagnostic information, or call external APIs. For instance, if a web server becomes unresponsive, SolarWinds can execute a PowerShell script to attempt a service restart, ping other nodes for comparison, or send a notification to an external escalation system. These scripts provide a flexible way to extend the response capabilities of the platform beyond passive alerting.

SolarWinds also integrates with **configuration management and automation tools** such as Ansible, Chef, Puppet, and SaltStack. Using the Orion API, these tools can query device status, push configuration changes, or adjust monitoring parameters based on the current state of the environment. For example, Ansible playbooks can retrieve node status from SolarWinds to determine if a server is active before applying updates, or automatically update device roles based on metadata pulled from the Orion database. This bidirectional integration allows monitoring to become part of the automation loop, enabling smarter decisions and reducing the risk of changes applied to unstable or offline systems.

Integration with **cloud platforms** like AWS and Microsoft Azure is also supported through APIs and templates designed to pull performance and usage data directly from cloud provider monitoring services such as CloudWatch and Azure Monitor. These integrations allow SolarWinds to display metrics such as CPU utilization, disk I/O, and network traffic from cloud-based virtual machines and services alongside on-premises infrastructure, providing a unified view of hybrid environments. API-based polling allows SolarWinds to retrieve data without requiring direct access to cloud-hosted instances, respecting cloud security boundaries while maintaining visibility.

For organizations leveraging **DevOps pipelines**, SolarWinds data can be integrated into CI/CD processes to provide feedback loops and gating mechanisms based on infrastructure health. Monitoring data can be used as input to decision-making logic that halts deployments if resource usage is high, restarts failed services before releases, or verifies environment readiness post-deployment. Data pulled from the SolarWinds API can be visualized in dashboards using tools like Grafana or integrated into Git-based workflows to trigger issue creation when anomalies are detected.

Another integration use case is with **data warehousing and analytics platforms**. Performance and availability data from SolarWinds can be exported to external databases or streamed into platforms such as Splunk, ELK Stack, or cloud analytics tools like BigQuery or Snowflake for advanced correlation, forecasting, or machine learning analysis. Custom scripts or API connectors can retrieve data on a schedule, normalize it, and load it into a central repository where it can be combined with logs, business KPIs, or user behavior metrics for deeper insights. This type of integration transforms monitoring from a reactive tool into a strategic data source for broader IT and business decision-making.

Authentication and user management integrations are also supported through Active Directory, LDAP, and SAML, allowing centralized control over user access and permissions within the Orion Platform. This makes it easier to manage user roles across tools and ensures consistency in access control policies. Integrating SolarWinds with identity providers improves auditability and enables features like single sign-on, multifactor authentication, and user provisioning workflows.

Integrating SolarWinds with security tools such as SIEM systems is another common practice. SolarWinds can forward syslog messages, SNMP traps, and alert data to systems like Splunk, QRadar, or ArcSight, where it becomes part of the broader security event landscape. This enables security teams to correlate configuration changes, availability events, and performance anomalies with threat intelligence and intrusion detection data, leading to more effective incident response.

The ability to integrate SolarWinds with a wide variety of systems and tools transforms it from a standalone monitoring solution into a central component of the IT operations ecosystem. Through APIs, webhooks, scripts, and platform connectors, SolarWinds bridges the gap between infrastructure monitoring, service management, automation, security, and analytics, ensuring that insights are not only visible but actionable across the organization. As environments continue to evolve, the extensibility of SolarWinds ensures that it can adapt and remain relevant in even the most dynamic and integrated IT landscapes.

Chapter 9: Security Considerations and Best Practices

Security considerations and best practices are critical components of any SolarWinds Orion Platform deployment, especially given the platform's ability to access, collect, and store sensitive information from across the IT infrastructure. A properly secured SolarWinds environment ensures that monitoring data remains confidential, system integrity is preserved, unauthorized access is prevented, and compliance with regulatory frameworks is maintained. Security must be addressed from multiple angles, including system hardening, user access control, network segmentation, encryption, update management, and auditing. The first step in securing a SolarWinds deployment is to follow a **principle of least privilege** approach, which involves granting users and service accounts only the minimum permissions necessary to perform their tasks. Within the Orion Web Console, role-based access control (RBAC) allows administrators to define custom roles and assign access rights to dashboards, nodes, reports, alerts, and administrative settings. This ensures that users only see and interact with the parts of the system relevant to their job, reducing the risk of accidental or malicious changes.

Integrating the Orion Platform with **Active Directory or LDAP** is recommended for centralized user authentication and streamlined identity management. This integration allows administrators to enforce group-based permissions, manage access through existing directory services, and simplify user provisioning and de-provisioning. For even stronger security, **multi-factor authentication (MFA)** should be implemented using an identity provider that supports SAML-based authentication. MFA adds a layer of protection beyond passwords, which are often vulnerable to compromise, and helps prevent unauthorized access to the monitoring system.

Securing the Orion Web Console itself involves several key steps. First, administrators should enforce **HTTPS for all web traffic** by installing valid SSL/TLS certificates and redirecting all HTTP requests to HTTPS. This ensures that all data transmitted between the web interface and the user's browser is encrypted, protecting against eavesdropping and man-in-the-middle attacks. Self-signed certificates should be avoided in production environments, and strong cipher suites should be enforced by configuring the underlying IIS web server. Additionally, the Orion Web Console should be restricted to specific management subnets or IP ranges through firewall rules or access control lists, minimizing the risk of external threats reaching the interface.

Database security is another essential consideration, as the Orion database stores configuration data, monitoring results, credentials, alert logs, and user information. The **SQL Server hosting the Orion database** should be configured to use encrypted connections, enforce strong authentication mechanisms, and follow best practices for database hardening. This includes disabling unused services, applying the latest security patches, using complex passwords for SQL accounts, and restricting administrative access to trusted users only. Backup files should also be encrypted and stored securely, ensuring that sensitive data is protected even in archived form.

Credential management within the Orion Platform must be handled with care, as SNMP community strings, WMI credentials, SSH keys, and cloud API tokens are used to access monitored systems. These credentials should be stored securely using **SolarWinds' encrypted credential management system**, which encrypts stored values using AES encryption with a rotating key. Administrators should periodically review and rotate credentials, especially after changes to staff or detected security events. Credentials should be scoped as narrowly as possible, and service accounts used for monitoring should have limited permissions, just enough to collect the required data without providing administrative access.

Network-level protections should also be in place, including **firewall segmentation**, intrusion detection systems (IDS), and virtual LANs (VLANs) to isolate the SolarWinds server, polling engines, and database from general user traffic. Only the necessary ports for Orion operations, such as HTTP/HTTPS, database ports, SNMP, and agent communication, should be opened between the relevant components, with all other ports blocked by default. Logging and monitoring of these network segments should be enabled to detect unusual activity, and tools like Security Information and Event Management (SIEM) systems should be integrated with SolarWinds to forward alerts and logs for centralized analysis.

Patch and vulnerability management is another best practice area that directly affects the security posture of a SolarWinds environment. All components of the platform— including the operating system, Orion modules, third-party dependencies, and web servers—must be kept up to date with the latest security patches. SolarWinds provides regular software updates that address vulnerabilities and introduce security enhancements, and administrators should follow the official release notes and apply patches promptly. In high-security environments, it is advisable to test patches in a staging environment before deploying them to production, ensuring compatibility while avoiding disruptions.

Audit trails and system logging are critical for accountability and forensic investigations. The Orion Platform includes detailed logging of user activity, configuration changes, login attempts, alert triggers, and system events. These logs should be reviewed regularly, stored securely, and retained according to the organization's compliance policies. SolarWinds can be configured to forward logs to external SIEM systems like Splunk, QRadar, or LogRhythm, where they can be analyzed for patterns, correlated with other security data, and used to generate alerts on suspicious behavior.

Least-privilege principles also apply to integrations and APIs. When using the **SolarWinds Orion SDK and REST API**, access tokens or credentials used by automation tools or external systems should be limited in scope and privilege. Only necessary API endpoints should be exposed, and access should be logged and reviewed. For example, a script that pulls node status should not be granted rights to create new users or delete configuration elements. IP-based restrictions, token expiration policies, and auditing of API usage all contribute to a more secure integration landscape.

Security best practices extend into backup and recovery planning. The Orion database and configuration files should be backed up regularly and tested for recoverability. Backups should be encrypted at rest and in transit, stored in secure locations, and protected by access controls. Recovery procedures should be documented and rehearsed so that if a compromise or failure occurs, the SolarWinds environment can be restored quickly without data loss or extended downtime.

In environments with compliance requirements such as PCI-DSS, HIPAA, or ISO 27001, SolarWinds can support audits by producing compliance reports, demonstrating data integrity, and enforcing security controls across infrastructure monitoring. Configuration baselines, change tracking, and system access logs all help demonstrate that the platform is secure, monitored, and managed according to industry standards. Regular internal audits, vulnerability scans, and penetration testing should be conducted to validate the effectiveness of security controls and uncover any potential weaknesses before they can be exploited.

By taking a comprehensive, layered approach to security and applying best practices across identity management, network access, configuration hardening, and monitoring integrations, organizations can ensure that their SolarWinds deployment is resilient, trustworthy, and ready to support both operational and compliance needs in today's complex IT environments.

Chapter 10: Optimizing SolarWinds for Enterprise Environments

Optimizing SolarWinds for enterprise environments requires a strategic approach that balances scalability, performance, security, and operational efficiency to ensure that the platform can handle the demands of large, distributed, and often complex IT infrastructures. Enterprises typically monitor thousands of devices, services, and applications across multiple data centers, cloud platforms, and remote locations, which makes careful planning and fine-tuning of the SolarWinds Orion Platform essential for sustained reliability and responsiveness. The first step in optimization begins with **proper sizing and architecture**, where decisions about the deployment model, database backend, polling engine distribution, and high availability setup must align with the current and projected monitoring load. SolarWinds provides sizing calculators and documentation to help determine whether a single-server deployment is sufficient or whether a distributed model with additional polling engines (APEs), web servers, and database servers is needed.

The core of any enterprise SolarWinds deployment is the **SQL Server database**, which stores configuration data, historical metrics, alert information, logs, and user interactions. Optimizing this database involves provisioning it on dedicated hardware or high-performance virtual infrastructure with sufficient CPU, memory, and especially fast disk I/O. Enterprises should use SQL Server Standard or Enterprise editions with the latest updates, and follow best practices such as separating database and transaction log files onto different storage volumes, configuring TempDB for concurrency, and allocating enough memory to SQL Server to cache frequently accessed data. The max server memory setting should be fine-tuned based on available system memory, and regular maintenance tasks such as index optimization, statistics updates, and database integrity checks should be automated to prevent long-term performance degradation.

Beyond the database, **polling distribution** is a key factor in enterprise-scale performance. Additional polling engines can be deployed to distribute the data collection load across geographic regions or high-volume segments of the infrastructure. Each polling engine can be assigned specific nodes or IP ranges, and careful balancing of node assignments ensures that no single engine becomes a bottleneck. Monitoring the performance of polling engines through internal SolarWinds metrics such as poller load, delay statistics, and job queue sizes allows administrators to fine-tune collection intervals, add new engines when thresholds are reached, and maintain consistent data freshness.

The **Orion Web Console**, which serves as the main interface for administrators and users, must also be optimized to deliver fast and responsive performance. In enterprise environments where many users access the console simultaneously, deploying additional web servers or enabling load balancing helps scale access and reduce latency. Caching, compression, and minimizing the number of widgets per dashboard view can also reduce server-side processing and speed up page loads. User roles and views should be configured to show only relevant data, avoiding large queries or overly complex dashboards that can slow down the interface.

Data retention policies play a major role in system performance and should be reviewed and adjusted based on organizational requirements. By default, SolarWinds retains raw historical data for 7 days and summarized trends for 30 days or longer, but in high-volume environments, these settings can lead to large database sizes and slower query performance. Adjusting the retention periods for event logs, syslogs, SNMP traps, and statistical data ensures that the system keeps only the necessary data for troubleshooting and reporting without bloating the database. Housekeeping jobs should be scheduled carefully and monitored to ensure they complete successfully without overlapping or impacting normal operations. Another key area of optimization is **alert tuning**, which involves reducing alert noise, eliminating redundant conditions, and prioritizing actionable events. In an enterprise context, thousands of alerts can be generated daily if thresholds are too sensitive or not aligned with business impact. Creating alert rules based on dynamic thresholds, custom properties, and business hours reduces false positives and ensures that teams are only notified when intervention is truly required. Grouping related alerts into correlated events, suppressing dependent alerts when a parent device is down, and implementing escalation policies based on severity and duration all contribute to more effective incident management.

Custom properties and dynamic groups provide powerful ways to organize devices and streamline monitoring at scale. Administrators can tag nodes based on criteria like location, environment (production, staging, test), application owner, or business unit, and then use those tags to drive dashboard views, alert scopes, and reporting logic. This approach simplifies delegation of monitoring responsibilities across teams and ensures that each team sees a customized view of the infrastructure relevant to their domain. Dynamic groups automatically include nodes based on matching criteria, which helps ensure that newly added devices are monitored and reported on without manual updates.

Integrating SolarWinds with **automation and orchestration platforms** further enhances enterprise optimization. Using tools such as Ansible, Puppet, or PowerShell, administrators can automate the addition of new nodes, assign templates, update custom properties, and adjust polling intervals in response to infrastructure changes. This reduces administrative overhead and ensures that the monitoring configuration remains in sync with actual infrastructure states. The SolarWinds API and Orion SDK enable such automation by allowing scripts and tools to interact programmatically with the platform, supporting tasks like bulk configuration changes, data extraction, or alert suppression during deployment windows.

Security considerations also form part of optimization, as performance must never come at the cost of protection. Implementing role-based access control, HTTPS encryption, encrypted credential storage, and secure communication between Orion components is essential in an enterprise setting. Audit logs should be reviewed regularly, and integration with SIEM platforms allows real-time security event correlation. Authentication via Active Directory or SAML providers simplifies user management and allows organizations to enforce existing identity policies across monitoring access.

Enterprises often require **compliance reporting and advanced analytics**, which means that the reporting engine in SolarWinds must be configured to generate and distribute meaningful, tailored reports. Scheduled reports should be scoped carefully using filters, groups, and custom properties to ensure relevance and reduce processing time. Export formats such as PDF and CSV can be used for external audits, and integration with business intelligence platforms like Power BI or Tableau allows deeper analysis when required.

In very large deployments, **High Availability (HA)** and disaster recovery (DR) become necessary. SolarWinds offers HA options for both the Orion server and SQL Server, using clustering, failover technologies, and replication to ensure continuous service during outages or maintenance. Backup strategies should include regular full database backups, configuration file exports, and documentation of recovery procedures. Testing DR plans periodically ensures that the organization can recover from incidents with minimal disruption.

Ongoing optimization requires continuous monitoring of the monitoring system itself. By using internal SolarWinds health metrics, administrators can keep track of polling delays, cache usage, query times, and system load, and make data-driven decisions about scaling or tuning. Alert thresholds, dashboard performance, and polling engine health should be reviewed regularly as infrastructure and monitoring needs evolve. By taking a proactive, systematic approach to performance, architecture, data retention, and operational integration, SolarWinds can serve as a high-performing, enterprise-grade monitoring solution capable of supporting critical infrastructure at any scale.

BOOK 3
SPLUNK ESSENTIALS
REAL-TIME INSIGHTS FROM MACHINE DATA

ROB BOTWRIGHT

Chapter 1: Introduction to Splunk and Machine Data Analytics

Introduction to Splunk and machine data analytics begins with understanding the growing importance of data generated by machines, applications, systems, networks, and sensors in modern IT and business environments. Every component in a digital ecosystem, whether it is a web server, firewall, router, virtual machine, mobile application, or IoT device, produces massive volumes of logs, events, metrics, and other telemetry. This information, often referred to as machine data, holds critical insights into the health, performance, usage, and security of infrastructure and applications. However, because this data is typically unstructured, high-volume, and time-stamped, extracting meaningful patterns and trends from it in real time poses a considerable challenge. This is where Splunk enters the picture as a powerful platform designed to collect, index, search, analyze, and visualize machine data from virtually any source in real time.

Splunk was originally developed to help IT administrators troubleshoot problems by searching through log files, but its capabilities have expanded far beyond that to support a broad range of use cases including security analytics, operational intelligence, application performance monitoring, business analytics, and compliance reporting. At the core of Splunk is its ability to ingest machine data in its raw form without requiring a predefined schema or transformation, making it highly flexible and adaptable to different data formats. Whether dealing with syslog messages, Windows Event Logs, application debug logs, SNMP traps, or sensor telemetry, Splunk can ingest the data, extract relevant fields, and make it searchable using its proprietary Search Processing Language (SPL).

The Splunk architecture is modular and scalable, consisting of several key components including the forwarder, indexer, search head, and deployment server. The **Splunk Universal Forwarder** is a lightweight agent that collects data from endpoints and forwards it securely to a central Splunk instance. It is optimized for minimal resource usage and can be deployed across thousands of systems. The **indexer** is the component responsible for receiving data, parsing it, applying indexing rules, and storing it in a searchable format. As data is indexed, Splunk assigns metadata such as source, source type, and host, making it easier to filter and query later. The **search head** is the interface through which users interact with Splunk, running searches, creating dashboards, setting alerts, and building reports. In larger environments, these roles can be distributed across multiple servers for scalability and performance.

Once the data is indexed, users can begin performing searches using SPL, a powerful query language designed specifically for working with machine data. SPL allows users to perform keyword searches, statistical aggregations, field extractions, time-based correlations, and conditional filtering, enabling deep and precise analysis. For example, a simple SPL query can find all failed login attempts within a specific time frame and group them by IP address to detect brute-force attacks. More complex queries can be used to calculate error rates, identify outliers, or correlate log entries from different systems. The results of SPL queries can be visualized using tables, charts, graphs, and gauges, which can be added to dashboards for continuous monitoring.

Splunk supports both real-time and historical data analysis, allowing teams to respond to incidents as they occur while also gaining long-term insights into trends and anomalies. Real-time searches power alerting workflows, where Splunk monitors for conditions like error spikes, policy violations, or unusual behavior and triggers actions such as sending an email, opening a ticket, or executing a remediation script. Historical analysis is useful for identifying root causes, performing capacity planning, generating audit trails, or evaluating service-level objectives. Splunk's time-series data model makes it especially effective at showing how metrics evolve over time and how changes in one part of the system affect others.

One of the major advantages of Splunk is its ability to handle data from multiple domains, making it a centralized analytics platform for DevOps, IT operations, security teams, and business users. For example, security analysts can use Splunk to detect unauthorized access, correlate threat indicators, and investigate breaches using data from firewalls, antivirus software, and identity providers. DevOps teams can use Splunk to monitor application logs, infrastructure health, deployment errors, and continuous integration pipelines. Business analysts can gain insights into customer behavior, website activity, transaction flows, and system availability, all using the same underlying data and tools.

Splunk offers a vast ecosystem of apps and add-ons that extend its functionality for specific vendors, technologies, and use cases. These include Splunk Enterprise Security (ES) for advanced threat detection, Splunk IT Service Intelligence (ITSI) for service health monitoring, and hundreds of integrations for cloud services, network devices, databases, containers, and SaaS platforms. These apps often include predefined dashboards, field extractions, and correlation rules, helping teams get value from their data more quickly. Splunk Cloud provides a fully managed SaaS version of the platform for organizations that prefer not to maintain their own infrastructure, offering the same capabilities with automated scaling, updates, and support.

Machine learning is another area where Splunk has built-in capabilities, allowing users to apply predictive analytics, anomaly detection, and forecasting to their data. With the Splunk Machine Learning Toolkit (MLTK), users can build and train models using SPL commands, apply algorithms like clustering, classification, and regression, and use these models to detect future patterns or deviations. For instance, a model could be trained to recognize normal behavior for a web application and trigger alerts when behavior deviates significantly from that baseline. These insights help organizations move from reactive monitoring to proactive management.

Data onboarding is simplified through Splunk's inputs and data onboarding assistant, which helps guide administrators through setting source types, field extractions, and index destinations. Once data is ingested and indexed, retention policies can be applied to control how long data is stored in hot, warm, cold, or frozen buckets, depending on the organization's storage and compliance needs. Splunk's distributed architecture ensures that it can scale horizontally as data volume increases, supporting high-ingest environments with load balancing and indexing clusters.

As machine data continues to grow in volume, velocity, and variety, tools like Splunk play an increasingly important role in helping organizations harness that data for operational efficiency, security, compliance, and business insight. By offering a flexible platform for ingesting, indexing, analyzing, and visualizing machine-generated data in real time, Splunk empowers teams to make data-driven decisions, detect issues faster, and turn raw logs into valuable intelligence across the enterprise.

Chapter 2: Installing and Configuring Splunk Enterprise

Installing and configuring Splunk Enterprise is the foundational step in setting up a powerful machine data analytics platform that enables organizations to monitor, search, analyze, and visualize data from a wide variety of sources. The installation process begins with understanding the system requirements, which include supported operating systems, hardware resources, and necessary dependencies. Splunk Enterprise can be installed on Windows, Linux, or macOS, though Linux is generally preferred for production environments due to its stability, performance, and scalability. Before installation, it is essential to ensure that the host system meets the minimum requirements, including sufficient CPU, RAM, disk space, and network bandwidth to handle the expected data ingestion volume and user activity.

The installation package for Splunk Enterprise can be downloaded directly from the official Splunk website after creating a free Splunk account. For Linux systems, Splunk provides a .rpm package for Red Hat-based distributions and a .deb package for Debian-based systems. Installation can be completed via the command line using tools like rpm -i or dpkg -i, while Windows users can use a standard executable installer with a graphical interface. During installation, administrators can choose the installation directory, set service account credentials, and configure whether Splunk should start automatically on system boot.

After installation, Splunk Enterprise runs as a service that listens on default ports—typically port 8000 for the web interface, port 8089 for management, and port 9997 for data forwarding. These ports should be opened in the system firewall if necessary. Once the service is running, the Splunk Web interface can be accessed through a browser by navigating to http://<hostname>:8000. The first login requires creating an administrator account by setting a username and password. This account provides full access to all Splunk features and is used to perform initial setup tasks.

Configuring Splunk Enterprise begins with **adding data sources**, which is one of the most important steps. Splunk supports a wide range of inputs including log files, system metrics, Windows event logs, network data via syslog, APIs, cloud services, and even streaming data from Kafka or MQTT. Data can be ingested using local file monitoring, scripted inputs, HTTP Event Collector (HEC), or via Universal Forwarders deployed on remote systems. The process of adding data is guided through the Splunk Web interface, where administrators can specify the data input type, set source types (which define the format and parsing rules), choose indexes for data storage, and configure host and metadata tagging.

Indexing is a critical part of how Splunk stores and retrieves data efficiently. When data is ingested, it is parsed, tokenized, and stored in time-based index buckets organized into hot, warm, cold, and frozen stages depending on age and access frequency. Splunk administrators should plan index strategies based on data retention policies, access patterns, and compliance requirements. Each index can be assigned specific size and time-based retention limits, as well as access permissions for role-based security. Creating dedicated indexes for different data types—such as security logs, application logs, or infrastructure metrics—can improve search performance and data organization.

Once data is being ingested and indexed, the next step is to **configure field extractions** and event parsing. Splunk uses predefined source types and regular expressions to extract key-value pairs from raw data, making it searchable and useful for analytics. Field extractions can be configured globally, within a specific app, or through inline search commands. Administrators can use the Field Extractor tool within the Splunk Web interface to define custom extraction rules without writing regular expressions manually. This is especially useful when dealing with custom log formats or non-standard data sources.

The **Search Processing Language (SPL)** is used to query, transform, and analyze the indexed data. SPL supports a wide range of operations including filtering, statistical aggregation, sorting, transaction correlation, and visualization. After installation, administrators can begin building saved searches, reports, and alerts that generate insights or detect anomalies in real time. Dashboards can be created to visualize key metrics using panels and widgets, allowing users to interact with data through time filters, drop-downs, and dynamic inputs.

Configuring **user roles and permissions** is an important task in securing Splunk Enterprise. The built-in roles include admin, power, user, and can_delete, each with predefined capabilities. Custom roles can be created to match organizational policies by assigning specific capabilities and limiting access to certain indexes, apps, or search functionalities. Integration with external authentication systems such as LDAP, Active Directory, or SAML-based identity providers enables centralized user management and supports single sign-on (SSO) for enterprise environments.

Another critical component of configuration is **setting up forwarders**, particularly the Splunk Universal Forwarder, which is a lightweight agent designed for data collection on endpoints. Universal Forwarders send data to Splunk indexers using secure, encrypted channels and support both Windows and Linux systems. Forwarders are installed separately and configured to monitor specific files, directories, event logs, or scripts. After installation, they must be pointed to the receiving indexer or heavy forwarder, typically using port 9997, and the indexer must be configured to accept forwarded data via the "Enable Receiving" setting.

Administrators should also configure **alerting** to monitor system conditions and detect potential issues. Alerts are saved searches that trigger actions when certain conditions are met, such as error spikes, failed login attempts, or infrastructure downtime. Alert actions can include sending emails, running scripts, posting to webhooks, or creating incidents in ITSM platforms. Thresholds and conditions can be defined using SPL, and alerts can be scheduled at fixed intervals or executed in real time.

For long-term success, **monitoring the health and performance** of the Splunk environment is essential. The Monitoring Console app, built into Splunk Enterprise, provides dashboards and reports that show indexing rate, search performance, resource usage, license consumption, and system alerts. This console is invaluable for identifying bottlenecks, forecasting growth, and troubleshooting configuration issues. It also helps maintain compliance with the assigned Splunk license, which is based on the volume of data indexed per day.

Splunk's **apps and add-ons** further extend the platform's capabilities by providing prebuilt dashboards, data inputs, and correlation rules for specific technologies such as AWS, Microsoft 365, Palo Alto, Cisco, and many more. These can be installed through the Splunkbase app store and configured to accelerate deployment in enterprise environments. Each app typically includes a technology-specific data model, enabling accelerated searches and integration with Splunk Enterprise Security or ITSI if those are part of the deployment.

Careful planning, structured configuration, and continuous tuning ensure that Splunk Enterprise performs optimally, scales with growing data volumes, and delivers real-time insights across the organization's digital infrastructure. From installation through to full deployment, each step builds the foundation for robust and intelligent machine data analytics.

Chapter 3: Data Inputs: Indexing Logs, Events, and Metrics

Data inputs in Splunk form the foundation of machine data analytics by enabling the platform to ingest and index logs, events, and metrics from a wide variety of sources, turning raw machine-generated data into actionable insights. Splunk is designed to accept data from virtually any source, regardless of its format or origin, which allows organizations to centralize monitoring across applications, infrastructure, security systems, and business operations. Whether it's traditional server logs, firewall events, application performance data, or metrics from cloud platforms, Splunk transforms this information into indexed, searchable records that support real-time analysis and long-term trend discovery.

The process of bringing data into Splunk starts with defining the input method. Splunk supports multiple input types including local file and directory monitoring, scripted inputs, Windows event logs, network data via TCP and UDP ports, HTTP Event Collector (HEC), and Universal Forwarders. For local file inputs, administrators can configure Splunk to watch directories or specific files for changes, ingesting new content as it is appended. This is ideal for logs generated by applications, web servers, or system daemons. Scripted inputs allow Splunk to run a script on a schedule, capturing the output and indexing it as event data. These are useful for collecting custom metrics, querying APIs, or extracting values from databases or command-line tools.

In Windows environments, Splunk can ingest **Windows Event Logs** and **Performance Monitor data**, offering deep visibility into system behavior, security logs, application crashes, and user activity. Event Log input types include Application, Security, System, and custom channels, which are specified in the Splunk Add-on for Windows. Performance Monitor counters allow collection of CPU usage, disk latency, memory pressure, and network statistics, all of which can be indexed as time-series metrics. On Linux and UNIX systems, similar capabilities are available using syslog, log file monitoring, and SNMP traps.

One of the most scalable and efficient methods of ingesting remote data is through the **Universal Forwarder**, which is a lightweight Splunk agent that collects and securely forwards logs, metrics, and scripts from endpoints to a central Splunk indexer. Universal Forwarders are commonly deployed on servers, virtual machines, and network devices, ensuring that logs are delivered in near real-time with minimal performance overhead. The forwarder supports encryption, load balancing, and routing logic, and can be centrally managed using deployment servers. This approach is preferred in enterprise environments where hundreds or thousands of devices need to report telemetry back to the Splunk platform.

For collecting data over the network, Splunk supports listening on **TCP and UDP ports** to receive syslog messages, SNMP traps, or application-generated messages. These inputs are often used to receive logs from routers, switches, firewalls, load balancers, and other appliances that support syslog as a standard output format. Syslog data can be noisy and high-volume, so administrators often configure filters or use heavy forwarders to parse and tag the data before indexing. Network input settings can be configured directly through the Splunk Web interface or via configuration files, specifying port numbers, source types, and target indexes. A more modern and API-driven input method is the **HTTP Event Collector (HEC)**, which allows applications and cloud services to send JSON-formatted events to Splunk over HTTP or HTTPS. HEC is ideal for use with microservices, containerized environments, and serverless architectures where agents cannot be deployed. Developers can instrument their applications to send telemetry directly to HEC endpoints, which can accept batched data, maintain source identity, and apply metadata tags such as host, source, and sourcetype. HEC tokens are generated within Splunk to authenticate the data source and can be configured with rate limits and access controls for security.

Splunk distinguishes between **events** and **metrics** during the indexing process. Events are typically unstructured or semi-structured logs that include time-stamped text messages generated by applications, systems, or devices. These are parsed and indexed as searchable entries with extracted fields. Metrics, on the other hand, are numeric time-series data such as CPU usage, request latency, or transaction rates, and are indexed into metric stores that are optimized for high-speed, low-latency aggregation. Splunk supports ingesting metrics in native format or converting events into metrics using transforms and field extractions.

Once data is ingested, Splunk assigns metadata such as **host**, **source**, and **sourcetype** to each event, which determines how the data is stored, parsed, and searched. The **host** identifies the origin of the data, such as a server name or IP address. The **source** refers to the input method or file path, and the **sourcetype** defines how Splunk interprets and extracts fields from the raw data. Properly assigning sourcetypes is essential for accurate parsing and consistent search behavior. Custom sourcetypes can be created for proprietary logs or modified to better suit specific data formats.

Administrators also configure **index destinations**, which determine where data is stored within Splunk. Indexes are logical partitions of the storage system, allowing for data separation, retention management, and access control. Different indexes can be created for categories such as security logs, application logs, infrastructure metrics, or compliance records. This organization enhances search performance and supports role-based access control by allowing certain users or apps to query only specific indexes.

Retention policies are defined at the index level and control how long data is retained before being deleted or archived. Splunk uses a tiered storage model consisting of **hot**, **warm**, **cold**, and **frozen** buckets. Hot and warm buckets are actively searchable, cold buckets are stored on less expensive storage media, and frozen data is removed or archived externally. Retention settings depend on the business requirements, compliance needs, and storage constraints of the organization.

In addition to indexing, data inputs can be enhanced through **props.conf** and **transforms.conf** files, which allow administrators to define advanced parsing rules, timestamp recognition, field extractions, event breaking, and data masking. These configurations are essential when dealing with complex or multi-line logs that require customized handling. Field extractions can also be performed at search time, giving users flexibility in how data is interpreted and visualized.

By supporting such a wide variety of inputs and formats, Splunk provides a flexible and extensible architecture for indexing machine data. Whether collecting logs from traditional IT infrastructure, streaming metrics from cloud-native applications, or ingesting events from security tools, the ability to define, route, tag, and manage data inputs effectively ensures that Splunk delivers accurate, timely, and actionable insights across the entire digital landscape.

Chapter 4: Building Powerful Search Queries with SPL

Building powerful search queries with SPL, or Search Processing Language, is central to unlocking the full potential of Splunk as a machine data analytics platform. SPL is a robust, purpose-built query language that allows users to retrieve, filter, transform, correlate, and visualize machine-generated data stored within Splunk indexes. Unlike traditional SQL used in relational databases, SPL is designed specifically for time-series event data, making it ideal for working with unstructured or semi-structured log entries, performance metrics, security events, and application telemetry. SPL queries begin with a data retrieval phase, which typically starts with a search command that specifies the index, source type, host, or other metadata fields to narrow down the scope of the data being queried. For example, a simple SPL query might look like index=web sourcetype=access_combined status=500, which returns all web access logs with HTTP 500 errors.

SPL allows for both keyword-based searches and more structured filtering using field-value pairs, wildcards, Boolean logic, and comparison operators. The search pipeline is constructed using a sequence of commands separated by the pipe (|) symbol, where the output of one command becomes the input for the next. This pipeline architecture enables users to chain together complex operations in a readable and modular fashion. One of the most commonly used commands in SPL is stats, which performs statistical aggregation on fields such as counts, averages, sums, and maximum or minimum values. For instance, | stats count by status would return a table of

HTTP status codes and their respective occurrence counts in the dataset.

Another powerful SPL command is timechart, which is used to generate time-series visualizations by aggregating values over time intervals. For example, | timechart span=1h count by status provides a line chart showing how different HTTP response codes trend over time in hourly intervals. The eval command allows for dynamic field creation and transformation, such as calculating response times in milliseconds, converting values to lowercase, or applying conditional logic. A common example is | eval load_category=if(cpu_load > 80, "high", "normal"), which creates a new field called load_category based on the value of the cpu_load field.

Field extractions and parsing are also critical when working with raw log data, and SPL supports a variety of commands to assist in this process. The rex command uses regular expressions to extract fields from within event data, which is especially useful when dealing with non-standard log formats or embedded JSON strings. For example, | rex "user=(?<username>\w+)" extracts the username value from log lines that contain a user field. The spath command is used to parse structured data like JSON or XML, enabling users to drill into nested fields and extract values using path notation. This is particularly important in modern environments where logs are often emitted in JSON format by microservices and cloud platforms.

Filtering and narrowing down search results is often achieved using the where command, which evaluates Boolean expressions and filters events accordingly. For example, | where duration > 1000 AND status="failure" returns only those events where the duration field exceeds 1000 and the status field equals "failure." For grouping related events, the transaction command can be used to correlate multiple log entries that share a common identifier, such as session ID or user ID, helping analysts understand the full sequence of actions during a session or incident.

SPL also includes commands for sorting (sort), deduplicating (dedup), joining data sets (join), looking up reference values (lookup), and appending additional results (append). For example, | dedup user_id ensures that only the most recent event per user is shown, while | lookup user_roles.csv user_id OUTPUT role enriches the data with role information from an external CSV file. The join command is used to combine datasets based on a shared field, such as linking authentication logs with access logs to investigate suspicious login activity.

Splunk also provides macro and tag capabilities that allow users to simplify complex queries or reuse query fragments across multiple dashboards and reports. Macros are named query snippets that can include parameters and are stored in configuration files, while tags allow for grouping related field values for more intuitive searching. These features are especially useful in large deployments where consistency and maintainability are important.

Visualizations are a core output of many SPL searches and can be built directly from search results using commands like table, chart, timechart, and geostats. The table command creates tabular reports that are easy to export or embed in dashboards, while geostats can be used to display event counts or metrics on geographic maps when location data is available. SPL also supports advanced visualizations through the use of drilldowns and dynamic tokens, allowing users to create interactive dashboards where selections from one panel influence the data shown in others.

Alerting is another key use case for SPL, where scheduled searches are defined with specific conditions that, when met, trigger automated responses. For example, | stats count by user | where count > 100 could be used to detect potential brute-force attacks and generate an alert when any user exceeds a threshold of login attempts. These alerts can be configured to send emails, call webhooks, execute scripts, or integrate with ticketing and security incident management systems.

The versatility of SPL extends to scheduled reports, data models, and accelerated datasets, where recurring queries are optimized for performance and integrated into high-level analytics tools like Splunk Enterprise Security or Splunk IT Service Intelligence. SPL is also used to build and manage knowledge objects such as event types, tags, and calculated fields, all of which contribute to a more contextual and insightful analytics environment.

By mastering SPL, users gain the ability to extract deep insights from complex and high-volume machine data, building powerful, flexible, and efficient searches that serve use cases across IT operations, security, compliance, and business intelligence. Each SPL command unlocks a different layer of understanding, and by combining them in creative ways, analysts can explore their data from multiple angles and make more informed decisions across the organization.

Chapter 5: Creating Interactive Dashboards and Visualizations

Creating interactive dashboards and visualizations in Splunk transforms raw machine data into insightful, accessible, and actionable views that empower users to monitor systems, detect issues, and explore trends without needing to write complex queries. Dashboards serve as the visual layer of Splunk, allowing different stakeholders to interact with data through a graphical interface tailored to their role, whether they are system administrators monitoring infrastructure, security analysts tracking incidents, or business users reviewing operational KPIs. The process of building a dashboard begins with designing a meaningful layout that reflects the type of data being displayed, the intended audience, and the key questions the dashboard needs to answer. Dashboards in Splunk are built using panels, each of which contains a visualization or data table backed by a search query written in SPL. These panels can include line charts, bar graphs, pie charts, single-value indicators, tables, maps, gauges, and more. Each panel can be resized and rearranged within the dashboard to emphasize high-priority metrics or display supporting context. For example, a dashboard monitoring web server performance might include a line chart showing request latency over time, a pie chart representing response code distribution, and a single-value panel displaying the current number of active sessions. These elements are powered by underlying SPL searches that return real-time or scheduled results, and their presentation can be customized using formatting options such as colors, fonts, legends, and tooltips.

Interactivity in dashboards is achieved through the use of **dynamic inputs**, which are UI elements that allow users to modify search parameters on the fly. Splunk provides several input types, including drop-down menus, multi-select lists, time pickers, radio buttons, checkboxes, and text boxes. These inputs are linked to tokens—placeholder variables that can be inserted into SPL queries or visualization configurations to update the dashboard based on user selections. For instance, a drop-down input listing server names could be tied to a token called $server$, which is then used in a panel's search like index=infra host=$server$. When a user selects a different server from the drop-down, the panel updates instantly to reflect data specific to that server.

Time pickers are particularly useful in dashboards, as time is a key dimension in almost all machine data analytics. Dashboards can include global time range pickers that affect all panels simultaneously or panel-specific time pickers for more granular control. Users can quickly switch between real-time monitoring, historical analysis, and custom date ranges without modifying SPL queries manually. This flexibility is valuable for incident investigation, trend analysis, or performance evaluation across different time periods.

Another important aspect of interactivity is **drilldown behavior**, which enables users to click on elements within a dashboard panel to trigger new searches, update other panels, or navigate to another dashboard. Drilldowns can be configured to pass values from a selected row, column, or chart segment into a token that modifies other panels or opens a more detailed view. For example, clicking on a bar in a chart showing failed login attempts by user can trigger a drilldown that filters a table to show all logs for that specific user during the selected time frame. This layered approach helps analysts move from summary to detail, speeding up root cause analysis and providing a more exploratory experience.

Splunk dashboards are defined using Simple XML, a declarative markup language that allows advanced customization of layout, behavior, and interaction. While the standard Dashboard Editor in the web interface offers a drag-and-drop experience for most users, administrators and power users can edit the XML directly to implement more sophisticated functionality such as conditional formatting, token chaining, custom JavaScript extensions, and HTML panels. By injecting HTML and CSS into dashboards, it is possible to apply custom branding, embed external content, or design highly tailored user experiences that align with organizational needs.

To support performance and usability, dashboards should be designed with efficiency in mind. Using **base searches** and **post-processing** allows multiple panels to share the results of a single query, reducing system load and speeding up page load times. For example, a base search that retrieves all error logs for the past 24 hours can feed several post-process searches that break down the results by application, severity, or source. This approach minimizes duplication and improves dashboard scalability, especially when working with high-volume indexes.

Splunk also supports scheduled searches and **summary indexing**, which allow frequently accessed dashboards to load faster by referencing precomputed results instead of running expensive real-time queries. Scheduled searches can populate summary indexes with aggregated data such as daily counts, averages, or top values, which are then used in dashboards for trend visualization or reporting. This is especially useful for executive dashboards or compliance reports that do not require minute-by-minute updates but must remain accurate and responsive.

The ability to export and share dashboards enhances collaboration across teams. Dashboards can be exported as static PDFs for executive briefings or compliance records, while links to live dashboards can be shared with team members who have appropriate access. Role-based permissions ensure that users only see the data they are authorized to access, maintaining data confidentiality while enabling organization-wide visibility. Splunk also supports embedding dashboards into other web applications or portals using iframe embedding or REST API integrations, which extends their reach beyond the Splunk platform.

Apps and add-ons available through Splunkbase often include prebuilt dashboards tailored to specific technologies such as AWS, Microsoft 365, Palo Alto, or Kubernetes. These dashboards provide out-of-the-box visualizations, field extractions, and drilldowns that accelerate deployment and reduce the need for custom development. Users can modify these templates to suit their environment or use them as inspiration for building new dashboards. As Splunk continues to evolve, newer dashboard frameworks like Dashboard Studio provide enhanced visual capabilities, drag-and-drop editing, and layout flexibility, making it easier for users of all skill levels to build engaging, informative, and interactive dashboards that bring machine data to life.

Chapter 6: Alerts, Scheduled Reports, and Real-Time Monitoring

Alerts, scheduled reports, and real-time monitoring in Splunk are essential components of an effective machine data analytics strategy, enabling proactive awareness, automated response, and continuous visibility into the health, performance, and security of IT systems. These capabilities transform Splunk from a reactive log analysis tool into a proactive monitoring platform that empowers organizations to detect issues before they escalate, automate responses to defined conditions, and deliver consistent operational reporting to stakeholders. The foundation of this functionality begins with **alerts**, which are based on saved searches that run at scheduled intervals or in real time and evaluate whether specified criteria are met. When a condition is triggered, Splunk can execute one or more alert actions to notify users, perform automated remediation, or integrate with external systems.

Creating an alert begins with crafting a precise SPL search that defines the event or condition to monitor. For example, a search such as index=auth sourcetype=linux_secure action=failure | stats count by user | where count > 5 might be used to detect brute-force login attempts by identifying users with more than five failed logins within a specified time window. After defining the search, users configure the alert conditions, which can include thresholds such as "greater than," "less than," "equal to," or more complex evaluations using custom logic. Alerts can be set to trigger when results are returned, when no results are found, or when statistical thresholds are crossed. The frequency of evaluation can be customized to run on a schedule—such as every 5 minutes—or continuously in real time for time-sensitive conditions. Once the alert condition is defined, Splunk offers a variety of **alert actions** that can be executed automatically when the alert fires. These actions include sending email notifications, posting messages to Slack or Microsoft Teams, executing custom scripts, logging events, creating incidents in IT service management tools such as ServiceNow or Jira, or triggering webhooks for integration with automation platforms. Email alerts can include search results, contextual information, and even dashboard screenshots, giving recipients immediate insight into the issue. Scripted actions can restart services, kill rogue processes, or adjust firewall rules based on the nature of the alert, enabling automated remediation workflows.

Alerting in Splunk also supports **throttling** and **alert suppression** to reduce noise and prevent repeated notifications for the same issue. For example, a CPU usage alert might be configured to trigger once every hour if the condition persists, rather than sending repeated emails every minute. Suppression settings allow alerts to be silenced for a defined period after firing or based on matching field values, such as only alerting once per host until the issue is resolved. This level of control ensures that alerts remain actionable and meaningful, reducing alert fatigue and helping teams focus on critical incidents.

In addition to alerts, **scheduled reports** are a powerful tool for automating the delivery of periodic insights and operational metrics to stakeholders. Scheduled reports are saved searches or dashboards that run at predefined intervals—daily, weekly, monthly, or on a custom schedule—and are emailed to recipients or stored in the Splunk file system. Reports can be formatted as PDFs, CSVs, or raw search results, and are often used to deliver compliance summaries, performance reviews, incident logs, or capacity planning data. For example, a weekly security report might summarize authentication failures, changes to privileged accounts, and firewall rule modifications across the environment. These reports help ensure that key stakeholders remain informed and can make data-driven decisions without needing direct access to the Splunk interface. Creating a scheduled report involves defining a search or dashboard, selecting the output format, and configuring the schedule and recipients. Reports can be sent to individual users, distribution lists, or external storage systems via scripts or API calls. Permissions can be applied to control who can create, view, or modify reports, ensuring that sensitive information is only accessible to authorized personnel. Templates can be used to maintain a consistent appearance across reports, and versioning can help track changes over time for audit purposes.

Real-time monitoring in Splunk takes advantage of the platform's ability to process and display data as it is ingested, allowing users to monitor system and application behavior with minimal delay. Real-time searches continuously evaluate incoming events and can be visualized on dashboards using live-updating panels, single-value indicators, and alert banners. These real-time visualizations are particularly valuable for use in network operations centers, security operations centers, and incident response teams that rely on immediate situational awareness. For example, a real-time dashboard might show failed login attempts as they occur, highlight spikes in 500-series HTTP errors, or display current network traffic rates per interface.

Splunk's **data models** and **accelerated data sets** can enhance real-time monitoring by enabling faster searches over large data volumes. When used in conjunction with summary indexing or report acceleration, dashboards and alerts can remain responsive even as data grows, ensuring that operational visibility is not compromised by scale. Real-time monitoring can also be supported by **base searches** and **post-processing searches**, which reduce system load by sharing a single search across multiple visualizations or alerts. Splunk's **notable events** and **incident review** features, available in premium apps like Splunk Enterprise Security, provide additional layers of context for real-time alerts. Notable events represent high-priority alerts that are automatically categorized and enriched with metadata, allowing analysts to track, triage, and investigate them within a unified incident review interface. Each event includes a timeline, affected assets, related threats, and user annotations, helping teams manage alert queues and collaborate effectively during incidents.

For environments that require integration with external monitoring and orchestration tools, Splunk supports alert actions that call REST APIs, generate SNMP traps, or send data to external dashboards and SIEM platforms. This flexibility allows Splunk to function as a central intelligence hub while feeding relevant alerts and insights into broader IT operations workflows. With properly tuned alerts, regularly scheduled reports, and responsive real-time monitoring, organizations can achieve a high level of observability, maintain system reliability, and act decisively when issues arise, all while reducing manual effort and enabling faster response across departments.

Chapter 7: Working with Apps and Add-ons

Working with apps and add-ons in Splunk extends the platform's core functionality by allowing users to tailor their environments to specific use cases, data sources, and operational needs. Apps and add-ons are modular components that package configurations, dashboards, field extractions, event types, saved searches, lookup tables, and sometimes scripts or binaries into a single unit that can be deployed across a Splunk environment. While both apps and add-ons provide additional capabilities, their purpose differs slightly. Apps are typically designed for interactive use by end users and include user interfaces, dashboards, and reports, whereas add-ons are more focused on data collection and normalization, acting behind the scenes to ensure that incoming data is properly structured and enriched.

The Splunk ecosystem is supported by Splunkbase, an online app store that offers thousands of free and paid apps and add-ons built by Splunk, partners, and community contributors. These packages accelerate time-to-value by providing prebuilt content tailored to specific technologies and platforms such as AWS, Microsoft 365, Cisco, Palo Alto Networks, Kubernetes, Salesforce, and many others. For example, the Splunk Add-on for Microsoft Windows collects and parses Windows event logs, performance counters, and registry data, while the Splunk App for AWS provides dashboards and visualizations for monitoring EC2 instances, S3 buckets, billing data, and CloudTrail logs.

Installing an app or add-on begins with downloading the package from Splunkbase or uploading a custom-built .spl file through the Splunk Web interface. Administrators can use the "Manage Apps" section in Settings to upload, enable, or disable apps and control permissions. Once installed, an app creates its own directory under $SPLUNK_HOME/etc/apps, where its configuration files, static assets, and modular components are stored. Apps are logically separated from one another, which allows developers to customize one app without affecting the rest of the Splunk deployment. This modularity also supports safe testing and version control of configurations and dashboards.

Add-ons often serve as the bridge between external systems and Splunk, particularly when dealing with data ingestion and field normalization. These packages typically include inputs to collect data, props and transforms to parse and reformat it, and tags or event types to aid in searching. For example, the Splunk Add-on for Cisco ASA includes pre-configured sourcetypes, field extractions, and CIM mappings that ensure firewall logs are correctly interpreted and usable in correlation searches. Most add-ons are designed to conform to Splunk's Common Information Model (CIM), a standardized data model that normalizes disparate data sources into a common schema. This enables correlation across technologies, supports accelerated searches, and allows data to be used effectively in apps such as Splunk Enterprise Security or Splunk IT Service Intelligence.

Working with CIM-compliant add-ons is essential in environments that rely on security and operational intelligence. When multiple data sources conform to CIM, users can run searches, build dashboards, or trigger alerts based on abstract field names like src, dest, action, or user, without needing to worry about the underlying log format. This consistency accelerates development and troubleshooting while ensuring compatibility with correlation rules, threat intelligence, and incident workflows. CIM mappings are defined in props.conf and transforms.conf files and are often tested using the datamodel and pivot interfaces in Splunk for validation and optimization.

Beyond installing and configuring apps, users and developers can build their own to address custom use cases. Splunk apps can include saved searches, macros, dashboards, custom visualizations, lookup tables, and alert actions, all organized in a way that can be easily shared or reused. Developers can use Simple XML for layout and UI logic or use the newer Dashboard Studio for more dynamic and visually rich interfaces. For more advanced functionality, apps can include Python or JavaScript scripts to enable modular inputs, REST handlers, or custom search commands. This extensibility allows Splunk to support advanced use cases such as anomaly detection, predictive maintenance, or fraud analysis.

Apps can also be deployed across **search heads, indexers, heavy forwarders, and universal forwarders**, depending on their purpose. A visualization app might be installed only on a search head, whereas a data collection add-on must be installed on the heavy forwarder or indexer responsible for ingesting that specific data. Splunk's deployment server can be used to manage app distribution across forwarders, ensuring that configuration changes are centrally managed and consistently applied across a large environment. For cloud-based deployments, Splunk Cloud supports a subset of vetted apps that are reviewed and certified for security and compatibility.

App and add-on configuration is managed through a combination of .conf files and the Web UI. Key configuration files include inputs.conf for data collection settings, props.conf for data transformation and field extraction, transforms.conf for routing and filtering, and outputs.conf for forwarding rules. These files can be manually edited or generated via the user interface, and changes are stored in the local directory of the app to preserve customizations across upgrades. Version control systems such as Git can be used to track changes in custom-built apps, and build pipelines can be created to test, package, and deploy apps programmatically.

Monitoring the performance and impact of apps is also important in large deployments. Some apps include introspection dashboards that provide metrics on search performance, memory usage, or indexing throughput. Splunk administrators can use the Monitoring Console to track app usage, search concurrency, and error messages related to specific app components. Keeping apps and add-ons updated is essential for security and compatibility, and vendors frequently release new versions that include support for updated APIs, new log formats, or CIM enhancements.

Apps and add-ons are what enable Splunk to be more than just a search engine for logs—they transform it into a highly adaptable, purpose-driven analytics platform that serves IT, security, DevOps, and business intelligence use cases with equal effectiveness. Whether enhancing the visualization layer, enabling specific data inputs, or extending platform capabilities with custom commands, apps and add-ons make Splunk customizable to the specific needs and goals of any organization. By leveraging and developing these modular components, users can create a unified and intelligent data experience that drives faster insight, smarter automation, and better decision-making across their digital ecosystem.

Chapter 8: Splunk Forwarders and Distributed Deployment

Splunk forwarders and distributed deployment architecture form the backbone of scalable, high-performance data ingestion and processing in large environments, enabling organizations to collect, transport, and index massive volumes of machine data from geographically distributed systems while maintaining centralized visibility and control. Splunk forwarders are lightweight software agents designed specifically to collect data from endpoints and securely transmit it to one or more Splunk indexers. There are two types of forwarders in Splunk: the **Universal Forwarder (UF)** and the **Heavy Forwarder (HF)**. The Universal Forwarder is a minimal, resource-efficient agent optimized for performance and reliability, capable of reading data from log files, event logs, and other sources and forwarding it in near real-time to a central indexing tier. It does not parse or index data locally, which reduces overhead on monitored systems and makes it ideal for broad deployment across servers, workstations, and devices.

The Heavy Forwarder, on the other hand, includes the full Splunk Enterprise instance and can parse, filter, and even index data locally if needed. It is typically used when data transformation or pre-processing must be performed before data reaches the indexer. Heavy Forwarders are used in scenarios where complex filtering rules are required, or where event routing must occur based on content. For example, in a secure environment, a Heavy

Forwarder might be used to mask sensitive data fields before forwarding the logs to the central indexer cluster. Because of its resource demands, the Heavy Forwarder is deployed selectively, while the Universal Forwarder is used extensively to scale collection across thousands of endpoints.

A **distributed Splunk architecture** is essential for enterprise-scale environments where data volumes and operational requirements exceed the capabilities of a single Splunk instance. In such deployments, the architecture is typically divided into three core tiers: the forwarder tier, the indexing tier, and the search tier. The forwarder tier consists of Universal and Heavy Forwarders that collect data from endpoints and applications. These forwarders can be configured to balance load across multiple indexers, provide failover in case of outage, and apply secure transport using SSL/TLS encryption to ensure data confidentiality in transit.

The indexing tier is composed of one or more **indexers**, which are Splunk Enterprise instances responsible for parsing incoming data streams, extracting fields, assigning metadata, and writing events to indexed storage. In large deployments, indexers are organized into **indexer clusters** that support high availability, replication, and horizontal scalability. An indexer cluster typically includes a **cluster master node** that manages peer indexers and oversees bucket replication and data consistency. Each incoming data event is written to multiple peer nodes to ensure durability and redundancy. Administrators can configure **replication factors** and **search factors** to define how many copies of data are maintained and how many are searchable, respectively.

The search tier consists of **search heads**, which provide the user interface and execute search queries across one or more indexers. In distributed environments, search heads are often deployed in **search head clusters** to provide scalability, high availability, and load balancing. A search head cluster consists of multiple search head nodes coordinated by a **deployer** and synchronized using a **replication mechanism** that ensures knowledge objects, such as dashboards, saved searches, and alerts, are consistent across the cluster. This design allows for seamless user access, failover support, and distributed query execution, which is critical in environments where hundreds of users and applications query Splunk data simultaneously.

Communication between forwarders and indexers is optimized using **load balancing**, which allows forwarders to distribute events across multiple indexers. This reduces the risk of overloading a single node and ensures more even utilization of indexing resources. Forwarders can be configured with a list of indexers, and they will rotate through these targets or distribute data based on a hash of the host, source, or sourcetype. In addition, Splunk supports **indexer acknowledgment**, a mechanism that confirms successful receipt and processing of data before the forwarder deletes the original log entry, ensuring reliable delivery and loss prevention.

Data flow in a distributed Splunk environment is often optimized using **intermediate forwarders**, particularly in multi-site or cloud-hybrid architectures. For instance, forwarders deployed on remote servers in a branch office can send data to a local Heavy Forwarder that pre-processes the data and forwards it to a regional data center. This approach reduces WAN bandwidth usage and centralizes data enrichment, routing, or masking logic. In cloud environments, forwarders can send data directly to **Splunk Cloud** or to on-prem indexers for further routing, depending on compliance and architecture requirements.

Deployment and management of forwarders at scale is streamlined using **deployment servers**, which allow administrators to define server classes and distribute configuration bundles to groups of forwarders automatically. This central management model ensures consistency in inputs, outputs, and monitoring configurations, and supports rapid onboarding of new systems. For example, a deployment server can be configured to push specific configuration files to all forwarders in a "Windows Servers" group, ensuring that each server sends Windows Event Logs and performance metrics to the correct index and sourcetype.

Security is a critical consideration in distributed deployments, and Splunk supports encrypted communication between forwarders and indexers using SSL certificates. Mutual authentication ensures that both sender and receiver are trusted, preventing man-in-the-middle attacks or data interception. In addition, role-based access control (RBAC) and index-level permissions are enforced at the search head to ensure that users can only query data relevant to their role or department.

Monitoring and troubleshooting in distributed environments are facilitated by the **Monitoring Console**, which provides insights into forwarder status, indexing performance, search concurrency, and license usage. Administrators can detect silent forwarders, indexer overload, delayed searches, and replication failures, allowing proactive resolution of issues that could affect performance or data availability. Splunk also provides REST API endpoints and logging mechanisms that can be used to audit, script, and automate common operational tasks across the deployment.

In summary, forwarders and distributed deployment form the scalable framework that allows Splunk to ingest data reliably from across the enterprise, route it securely and efficiently, and index it in a way that supports fast, distributed searches. By leveraging Universal and Heavy Forwarders, indexer clusters, search head clusters, and deployment servers, organizations can build robust monitoring and analytics infrastructures that scale with their data and support diverse operational, security, and compliance needs.

Chapter 9: Security and Access Control in Splunk

Security and access control in Splunk are fundamental components of any deployment, ensuring that data is protected from unauthorized access, that user activity is monitored and auditable, and that the platform complies with organizational policies and regulatory requirements. As a centralized platform for collecting and analyzing vast amounts of machine data—including logs from servers, firewalls, applications, cloud services, and security systems—Splunk must be tightly secured both at the platform level and within the data itself. Access control in Splunk starts with authentication, which determines how users prove their identity to the system. Splunk supports several authentication methods including native Splunk authentication, LDAP or Active Directory integration, SAML-based single sign-on (SSO), and multifactor authentication through external identity providers.

Native authentication is typically used in test or small environments and involves managing usernames and passwords directly within Splunk. For enterprise environments, LDAP or Active Directory integration is preferred, as it allows centralized control over user accounts and supports group-based mapping to Splunk roles. When configured, LDAP authentication allows Splunk to query the directory service to verify credentials and assign users to predefined roles based on their group membership. SAML integration allows organizations to enforce single sign-on using identity providers such as Okta, Azure AD, or Ping Identity, streamlining the user login experience while also enabling multifactor authentication and session policies.

Once authenticated, access control in Splunk is enforced through **role-based access control (RBAC)**. Every user in Splunk is assigned to one or more roles, and each role defines a set of capabilities and index permissions that govern what the user can see and do within the platform. Capabilities include permissions such as running searches, editing alerts, managing apps, deleting events, or viewing field extractions. Index permissions determine which data the user can access, allowing administrators to isolate sensitive data such as security logs or financial records from general users. For example, a helpdesk user might have a role that grants read access only to authentication and workstation logs, while a security analyst might have broader access to all security-related indexes.

Roles can be customized to suit organizational needs and can inherit capabilities from other roles, allowing for efficient configuration and granular control. Best practice involves creating roles aligned with job functions—such as SOC analyst, IT administrator, compliance auditor—and mapping LDAP groups to those roles so that access is automatically assigned based on directory membership. This reduces administrative overhead and ensures that access is provisioned and revoked according to the organization's identity management lifecycle.

Beyond roles and capabilities, Splunk provides additional control over **search constraints and data visibility** through knowledge objects such as event types, tags, macros, and workflow actions. Search filters can be applied to roles to restrict access to certain events, even if the user has index-level permissions. For instance, a search filter could prevent a role from accessing events that contain specific keywords or source types. This allows for more nuanced control over data exposure and supports compliance with privacy policies such as GDPR or HIPAA.

Audit logging is a critical aspect of security in Splunk, allowing administrators to track user actions, configuration changes, and system events. The internal logs generated by Splunk record activities such as logins, failed authentication attempts, search executions, role changes, and app installations. These logs can be indexed and monitored like any other data source, enabling the creation of dashboards and alerts that track administrative behavior, detect suspicious patterns, or enforce change control policies. For example, an alert can be configured to notify security personnel when a new user role is created or when a user attempts to access restricted indexes.

Encryption is another core component of Splunk security. Communication between forwarders, indexers, and search heads can be encrypted using SSL/TLS to prevent eavesdropping and man-in-the-middle attacks. Splunk supports mutual TLS authentication, where both client and server present certificates to verify each other's identity, enhancing trust in distributed environments. In addition to encrypting data in transit, Splunk also supports encryption of **data at rest** through the use of file system encryption mechanisms or integration with encrypted storage platforms. Sensitive data such as stored credentials, certificates, and secrets are encrypted within Splunk using AES-256 encryption, and administrators can rotate encryption keys as part of standard security hygiene.

Splunk's **HTTP Event Collector (HEC)** also supports token-based authentication and can be secured with SSL to ensure that data ingestion via HTTP is both authenticated and encrypted. Each HEC token can be configured with specific source types, indexes, and permissions, allowing fine-grained control over which sources are allowed to send data and where that data is stored. HEC tokens can be revoked or rotated as needed, supporting strong security practices in environments where many external applications report into Splunk.

Security in Splunk extends to its app ecosystem as well. Apps and add-ons should be sourced from trusted developers and reviewed for security risks before installation. Splunkbase provides verified and vetted apps, and administrators can control which apps are allowed in production environments. Installed apps run within the Splunk environment and may execute scripts or perform system operations, so controlling permissions and reviewing configurations is essential to maintaining a secure posture. For organizations using Splunk Cloud, additional protections and automated checks are in place, including regular vulnerability scanning, configuration validation, and app vetting to ensure customer data remains secure.

Administrators can also enforce **session security policies**, such as session timeouts, idle time limits, and login attempt thresholds, to prevent unauthorized access via stale or hijacked sessions. Login activity can be monitored, and suspicious behaviors—such as repeated failed attempts or logins from unusual IP ranges—can trigger alerts or automated remediation workflows. Splunk also provides guidance and tooling for compliance with standards such as NIST, PCI-DSS, ISO 27001, and CIS, enabling organizations to align their deployment with established security frameworks.

In multitenant or departmental environments, **data segmentation and app access control** help isolate data and interface elements across teams. Apps can be scoped to specific roles, and dashboards can be restricted so that users only see content relevant to their responsibilities. This not only improves security but also enhances usability by removing unnecessary complexity from the user experience.

Maintaining security in Splunk is an ongoing process, requiring regular reviews of roles, user activity, app configurations, and system settings. Security best practices include applying updates promptly, using the Splunk Monitoring Console to track system health and access activity, and regularly auditing configuration files for unauthorized changes. By implementing strong authentication, granular access control, encrypted communications, and comprehensive audit logging, Splunk provides a secure and flexible platform for managing critical machine data across the enterprise.

Chapter 10: Optimizing Performance and Troubleshooting

Optimizing performance and troubleshooting in Splunk are essential practices for maintaining a fast, responsive, and reliable environment that can scale with increasing data volumes and user demands. As Splunk is deployed across larger infrastructures and used by more users, performance optimization becomes increasingly important to ensure that searches return results quickly, dashboards load smoothly, and alerts are generated in a timely manner. The first step in performance optimization is understanding how Splunk processes data during indexing and searching. During indexing, data is ingested, parsed, and stored in time-based index buckets, while during search, the system reads from those buckets and performs field extractions, calculations, and visualizations based on the search processing language (SPL). Any delay or inefficiency in these processes can lead to degraded user experience or missed operational signals.

One of the key areas to focus on is **search optimization**, as poorly constructed SPL queries can consume excessive system resources, delay results, and negatively impact other users on the same deployment. Long-running or inefficient searches often stem from wildcard usage in the index, sourcetype, or host fields, failure to use time range restrictions, or unnecessary post-processing commands. To improve search performance, users should always define the narrowest possible time window and use specific index and sourcetype values to limit the scope of the search. For example, replacing a generic index=* with index=web sourcetype=access_combined can reduce the number of scanned events significantly. Using fields or table commands to limit returned fields and avoiding expensive commands like join, transaction, and append unless strictly necessary also helps improve search efficiency.

The **Search Job Inspector** is a built-in tool in Splunk that provides deep insights into search performance by showing detailed metrics such as execution time, scanned events, index access time, and command breakdowns. By analyzing these metrics, administrators and users can pinpoint which part of a search is causing bottlenecks and take corrective action. For example, if most of the time is spent on the stats command, it may indicate a large number of distinct values being processed, which can be reduced through filtering or summarization techniques.

Indexing performance is another critical factor that can affect the overall system. Splunk writes data to disk in **index buckets** that progress through different stages: hot, warm, cold, and frozen. Each stage has its own storage and performance implications. Administrators should ensure that the indexers are equipped with fast disk subsystems, such as SSDs, especially for hot and warm buckets that are frequently read and written. Disk I/O contention, insufficient memory, or CPU saturation on indexers can lead to indexing delays and search lag. Monitoring these hardware metrics through the **Monitoring Console** allows early detection of performance issues and supports capacity planning.

Summary indexing is a powerful technique used to improve performance for recurring, long-running searches that involve large datasets. It works by running a scheduled search at regular intervals and writing the summarized results to a new index, which can then be queried instead of the raw data. This significantly reduces the amount of data that needs to be processed at search time, resulting in faster dashboards and reports. Summary indexing is particularly useful for KPIs, trend analysis, and reporting scenarios that do not require real-time granularity.

Splunk also supports **report acceleration** and **data model acceleration**, which speed up access to large datasets by creating pre-computed summaries. These features are especially useful in environments using **pivot tables**, **data models**, or **Splunk Enterprise Security**. Acceleration settings should be carefully managed, as they consume system resources and require periodic rebuilding to stay up to date. Administrators should regularly review and tune acceleration policies to align with user needs and available system capacity.

Another performance optimization area is managing **concurrent search limits** and **scheduler load**. Splunk has predefined limits on the number of concurrent scheduled and real-time searches to prevent overload. When these limits are exceeded, searches may be skipped or delayed, which affects dashboards and alert reliability. The **Search Scheduler Activity** dashboard in the Monitoring Console helps identify skipped searches and shows which users, apps, or searches are consuming the most resources. Administrators can use this information to reschedule heavy searches to off-peak times, adjust priority levels, or break complex searches into smaller components.

When troubleshooting performance issues, it's essential to check system logs such as splunkd.log, scheduler.log, and metrics.log for error messages, timeouts, or hardware warnings. These logs provide insight into failed searches, queue delays, indexing slowdowns, and other operational anomalies. For distributed deployments, network latency or misconfigured load balancing between forwarders and indexers can also affect performance. Ensuring that **forwarders are load balanced** properly and that **index replication** settings are optimized prevents bottlenecks and maintains indexing throughput.

In environments with large numbers of forwarders, administrators should monitor forwarder connectivity using the **Forwarder Management** interface or the **Deployment Monitor** app. These tools can help detect silent or misconfigured forwarders, verify data transmission rates, and troubleshoot dropped or delayed data. If specific forwarders are not sending data or experiencing queue buildup, reviewing splunkd.log on those endpoints and checking firewall or network settings can often reveal the root cause.

App and dashboard performance can also affect the user experience. Dashboards with too many panels, excessive real-time components, or unoptimized base searches can slow down page loads and increase server load. Best practices include limiting the use of real-time panels, using **post-processing searches** wherever possible, and designing dashboards to load incrementally or on user input. The **Dashboards Performance** dashboard in the Monitoring Console can help identify dashboards that are consuming high CPU, memory, or search slots, allowing developers to refactor them for efficiency.

Resource management is another key consideration, and Splunk administrators should regularly monitor **license usage**, **disk space**, and **CPU/memory** utilization across all nodes. Setting thresholds and alerts for these metrics ensures that action can be taken before problems affect performance. Splunk also allows setting quotas for user roles, such as limiting the number of concurrent searches or maximum search runtime, which prevents individual users or apps from monopolizing system resources.

Scaling out Splunk infrastructure by adding **indexers, search heads, or forwarders** is often necessary as data volumes grow. Horizontal scaling, combined with good data onboarding practices and intelligent search design, allows organizations to maintain high performance even as data sources and users increase. Load balancing, indexer clustering, and search head clustering should be implemented and regularly reviewed to ensure even distribution of load and fault tolerance.

By continuously monitoring system health, optimizing searches, managing infrastructure resources, and applying best practices for search design and indexing, Splunk environments can achieve high performance, rapid troubleshooting capabilities, and reliable delivery of insights across the organization.

BOOK 4
CACTI IN ACTION
VISUAL NETWORK MONITORING MADE SIMPLE

ROB BOTWRIGHT

Chapter 1: Getting to Know Cacti: What It Is and Why It Matters

Getting to know Cacti begins with understanding that it is a robust, open-source network graphing and monitoring tool designed to harness the power of RRDTool, a data logging and graphing system for time-series data such as network bandwidth, CPU load, memory usage, and system temperatures. Cacti serves as a complete frontend solution for collecting, storing, and displaying performance metrics through intuitive, customizable graphs and dashboards. It is widely used by network administrators, system engineers, and IT professionals to gain visibility into the health and behavior of devices and services across their infrastructure. Cacti's value lies in its ability to provide detailed, real-time and historical insights that help detect anomalies, ensure uptime, and support capacity planning without requiring expensive commercial solutions.

Cacti is built around the concept of polling data at regular intervals using SNMP, scripts, or custom queries, storing the results in round-robin databases (RRDs), and generating graphs based on this data. The round-robin database format is particularly well-suited for long-term data retention because it stores data in a fixed size, rotating older entries out to make room for new ones without increasing disk usage. This makes Cacti ideal for environments where historical performance trends need to be tracked over months or years. By default, Cacti provides built-in templates for graphing standard metrics like traffic on router interfaces, but its extensible architecture allows users to define custom data sources, templates, and scripts to monitor virtually any measurable parameter.

One of the key reasons Cacti matters in a modern IT environment is its lightweight and efficient design. It does not require massive infrastructure to run and can be deployed on modest hardware or virtual machines, making it accessible to organizations of all sizes. The Cacti web interface allows administrators to manage devices, configure data sources, set polling intervals, create graphs, and organize them into hierarchical trees for easy navigation. This centralized interface ensures that even users with minimal background in network monitoring can view and interpret system performance at a glance.

Cacti's support for SNMP (Simple Network Management Protocol) enables it to poll data from a wide variety of network hardware such as switches, routers, firewalls, and printers, as well as servers and storage systems. SNMP polling retrieves metrics like input/output traffic, CPU load, disk space, temperature sensors, and interface status, which can be visualized in real-time. Because SNMP is a vendor-neutral protocol, Cacti can operate in diverse environments without being locked into a single ecosystem. In addition to SNMP, Cacti supports custom scripts written in languages like Bash, Python, or Perl, which can be used to collect metrics from log files, databases, APIs, or other sources that do not expose SNMP endpoints.

Cacti matters because it enables proactive monitoring, which is critical in preventing downtime and minimizing the impact of performance issues. By collecting and visualizing time-series data, administrators can spot patterns and correlations—such as bandwidth saturation during specific hours, increased CPU usage during backups, or declining available disk space—which may indicate emerging problems. Graphs in Cacti are not just static charts; they can be used to support root cause analysis, validate configuration changes, and demonstrate service-level trends over time. With customizable alerting through plugins and third-party integrations, Cacti can also notify administrators when metrics exceed defined thresholds, enabling faster response times and better operational continuity.

Another aspect that makes Cacti valuable is its **template system**, which streamlines the process of monitoring similar devices or systems. Instead of manually configuring each data source and graph for every device, administrators can apply templates that automatically define what to monitor and how to visualize it. This saves time and ensures consistency across the environment. For example, a template for Cisco switches might include graphs for port bandwidth, errors, and CPU usage, and it can be applied to all switches of that type with just a few clicks. Cacti's templates can be exported and shared, supporting collaboration and best practice sharing within the community.

Cacti's plugin architecture enhances its core capabilities by adding features such as user authentication with LDAP or Active Directory, device discovery, advanced alerting, reporting, syslog integration, and more. The Spine poller, a high-performance data collector written in C, can be used as an alternative to the default PHP poller for larger environments, significantly improving polling efficiency and scalability. This flexibility means that Cacti can grow alongside the organization, adapting to increasing demands without requiring a migration to a new platform. Security is also a consideration, and Cacti supports role-based access control, ensuring that users can be granted permissions based on their responsibilities. For example, a network technician might only have access to view specific graphs, while a system administrator can modify polling settings and manage devices. The user interface is logically structured, with tabs and menus that make navigation intuitive, even in deployments with hundreds of monitored devices.

Because Cacti is open source, it benefits from continuous community development and support. Its active user and developer community contribute bug fixes, feature enhancements, and updated templates for emerging technologies. Documentation, forums, and wikis provide extensive resources for troubleshooting, customization, and learning best practices. This community-driven model ensures that Cacti remains a viable and competitive solution in a landscape filled with both open-source and proprietary monitoring tools.

Cacti plays an important role in environments where visibility, reliability, and historical context are crucial. Whether used in small office networks, large enterprises, or service provider infrastructures, Cacti provides the insight necessary to make informed decisions, track usage patterns, and justify upgrades. With its ability to transform raw metrics into meaningful graphs, its support for diverse data sources, and its highly customizable interface, Cacti serves as a vital tool for IT teams seeking a cost-effective yet powerful monitoring solution.

Chapter 2: Installation and Initial Configuration

Installation and initial configuration of Cacti is a structured process that involves preparing the environment, installing necessary software packages, configuring the database, and setting up the web interface so that Cacti can begin collecting and graphing data from devices across the network. Because Cacti is a web-based application built on PHP, it requires a LAMP or LEMP stack—Linux, Apache or Nginx, MySQL or MariaDB, and PHP. The first step is selecting the appropriate operating system, with most users choosing a Linux distribution such as CentOS, Ubuntu, Debian, or Rocky Linux for its stability and compatibility. Before beginning the installation, system administrators should ensure that the server is updated with the latest packages using the system's package manager, such as apt or yum.

Next, the required software packages must be installed. This includes a web server like Apache or Nginx, a relational database server such as MySQL or MariaDB, PHP along with required extensions like php-mysql, php-snmp, php-xml, php-gd, and php-mbstring, as well as RRDTool, which Cacti uses to store and graph time-series data. Depending on the distribution, these packages can be installed using a single command, for example apt install apache2 mariadb-server php php-mysql rrdtool snmp php-snmp on Debian-based systems. It is important to configure PHP settings to meet Cacti's requirements, such as increasing memory limits and execution timeouts in the php.ini file to handle graph rendering and polling operations.

Once the necessary software stack is in place, the next step is to create a MySQL or MariaDB database and user account for Cacti. This is typically done by logging into the database server with root privileges and executing a series of SQL commands to create the database, assign a user, and grant appropriate permissions. For example, commands such as CREATE DATABASE cacti;, CREATE USER 'cactiuser'@'localhost' IDENTIFIED BY 'securepassword';, and GRANT ALL PRIVILEGES ON cacti.* TO 'cactiuser'@'localhost'; prepare the database environment. After the database is created, it must be initialized with the schema provided by the Cacti installation package, which includes tables for devices, data sources, user accounts, templates, and settings.

Cacti can be downloaded from its official website or installed through the package manager if the distribution provides an up-to-date version. Manual installation provides more flexibility and ensures the latest stable version is used. Once the package is extracted into the web server's document root—typically /var/www/html/cacti—the correct ownership and permissions should be applied to allow the web server to read and write to the necessary files and directories. This is usually accomplished with commands such as chown -R www-data:www-data /var/www/html/cacti on Debian-based systems.

Cacti's web-based installer is used to perform the initial configuration and guide the user through setting up the application. When accessing the installation URL in a browser, such as http://server-ip/cacti, the installer checks system prerequisites and prompts the user to supply database connection details, including the database name, username, and password. The installer also verifies that PHP modules, file permissions, and system binaries like RRDTool and snmpwalk are available. After successfully connecting to the database and initializing the schema, the installer continues with setting up the administrator account, timezone configuration, and basic SNMP settings.

Once installation is complete, Cacti will prompt the user to log in with the default administrator credentials, which can be changed immediately for security purposes. Upon first login, the Cacti dashboard presents a basic layout that includes the main menu, graph viewing section, and configuration panels. From here, the user should proceed to configure the poller, which determines how data is collected from monitored devices. By default, Cacti uses the PHP-based poller, but for larger environments, it is recommended to switch to Spine, a multithreaded poller written in C for better performance. Spine can be compiled from source or installed via package manager and must be configured in Cacti's settings to replace the default poller engine.

The next phase of configuration involves adding devices to monitor. Devices such as routers, switches, servers, and printers can be added through the web interface by navigating to Devices → Add. For each device, the user specifies a hostname or IP address, SNMP version and community string, device type, and associated templates. Cacti supports SNMP v1, v2c, and v3, and for security-conscious environments, SNMPv3 is recommended due to its support for authentication and encryption. After a device is added, Cacti automatically queries it to determine available interfaces and metrics, which can then be used to create graphs.

Graph creation is handled through templates, which define how data sources are visualized. Users can apply predefined templates or create custom ones by specifying data input methods, graph items, colors, and display formats. These templates make it easy to consistently monitor similar devices. Once graphs are created, they appear in the graph tree, which can be customized to group devices by function, location, or department. This organization makes it easier to navigate large deployments and provides quick access to the most critical views.

Basic user roles and permissions should also be configured early in the deployment to ensure secure access. Cacti supports multiple user accounts with customizable permissions, allowing administrators to control who can view, edit, or add devices and graphs. Role-based access control helps enforce operational boundaries, particularly in environments where multiple teams share responsibility for different parts of the infrastructure.

Initial configuration also involves tuning polling intervals, adjusting retention settings, and enabling logging. Cacti's default polling interval is five minutes, which balances granularity and system load. For high-frequency data collection, this can be lowered, though it requires corresponding adjustments to RRD file configurations. Logging should be enabled to track polling failures, SNMP errors, and authentication issues, which are invaluable during troubleshooting and performance analysis. With these initial steps completed, Cacti is ready to begin collecting data and providing valuable insights through its intuitive visualizations and reporting capabilities.

Chapter 3: Working with SNMP and Data Sources

Working with SNMP and data sources in Cacti is a fundamental aspect of configuring the platform to monitor networked devices and collect time-series data for performance graphing and analysis. SNMP, which stands for Simple Network Management Protocol, is a widely used protocol that enables the retrieval of metrics and operational data from hardware devices such as switches, routers, firewalls, wireless access points, printers, and servers. Cacti leverages SNMP to perform polling operations, which involve sending requests to SNMP-enabled devices at regular intervals to collect numerical values associated with various metrics. These values are stored in RRDTool databases and visualized through graphs, giving administrators insight into system behavior over time. The first step in working with SNMP in Cacti is ensuring that devices are configured to support SNMP communication. Most enterprise-class network and server hardware includes built-in SNMP agents that can be enabled and configured via the device's management interface. These agents respond to SNMP requests and expose data through a hierarchical structure known as the Management Information Base, or MIB. Each entry in the MIB is identified by an Object Identifier (OID), which represents a specific piece of information such as CPU usage, network interface traffic, or system uptime. SNMP operates in different versions, including SNMPv1, SNMPv2c, and SNMPv3. SNMPv1 and v2c are widely used and simple to configure, relying on a community string for authentication. SNMPv3 adds enhanced security features including authentication and encryption, making it the preferred choice for secure environments.

In Cacti, adding an SNMP-enabled device involves navigating to the Devices section in the web interface and specifying the device's IP address or hostname, SNMP version, community string (or credentials for SNMPv3), and device type. Cacti then performs a discovery process using SNMP to identify what metrics are available from the device. If successful, the device's system information, such as hostname, uptime, and description, is displayed, confirming that SNMP communication is working. Administrators can then proceed to associate graph and data query templates with the device, enabling the automatic creation of graphs for commonly monitored statistics. Data sources in Cacti serve as the link between the raw data retrieved from SNMP and the graphical representation of that data. Each data source defines how a specific metric is polled, stored, and processed. Cacti supports several types of data sources, with SNMP being the most common, but also including script-based sources and advanced data collection methods such as those used by plugins. When creating or editing a data source, users configure attributes such as the polling method (SNMP, script, etc.), the OID or script path, the expected data type (gauge, counter, or derive), the data source name, maximum and minimum values, and the step interval, which defines how frequently the data is updated.

Understanding how SNMP data types work is essential for accurate data collection. SNMP counters, such as those used for interface traffic, continually increase until they roll over. Cacti automatically calculates the rate of change between polling intervals to determine metrics such as bits per second. Gauges, on the other hand, represent absolute values like temperature or CPU load and do not require rate calculations. Cacti's ability to interpret these data types correctly is critical for ensuring that graphs display meaningful values. For example, incorrect configuration of a counter as a gauge would result in misleading data that could suggest traffic drops or spikes where none exist. Templates play a crucial role in simplifying the use of SNMP and data sources across multiple devices. Cacti's data input methods and graph templates can be combined into device templates that encapsulate all the required SNMP queries and graph definitions for a specific type of hardware. For example, a Cisco switch template might include SNMP queries for interface bandwidth, error rates, and CPU usage, along with preconfigured graph formats. By applying this template to a newly added Cisco device, administrators can generate dozens of relevant graphs in seconds without having to manually define each data source and graph item. This approach streamlines monitoring configuration and ensures consistency in how data is collected and visualized. Cacti also allows the creation of custom SNMP data queries using the SNMP Query Wizard, which assists users in defining new OIDs to monitor when a specific metric is not already covered by existing templates. This is particularly useful when working with specialized hardware or software systems that expose unique metrics through their MIBs. The wizard guides the user through selecting an OID, choosing the data type, and testing the SNMP response from the target device. Once configured, the new data query can be reused across devices, incorporated into templates, and associated with graphs.

For more advanced scenarios, administrators may need to use external tools like snmpwalk or snmpget to browse the MIBs of target devices, identify OIDs of interest, and verify SNMP responses. These command-line tools are invaluable for troubleshooting SNMP connectivity issues, verifying credentials, and locating undocumented OIDs. Once an OID is identified, it can be integrated into Cacti's data collection framework by defining a new data input method and associating it with a graph template.

Poller configuration is another important aspect of working with SNMP in Cacti. The poller is responsible for executing all data collection tasks at scheduled intervals, typically every five minutes. Cacti's default PHP-based poller is suitable for smaller environments, but for larger networks with hundreds or thousands of SNMP targets, using Spine as a poller is recommended. Spine is multithreaded and written in C, offering significantly better performance and reduced poll times. Poller performance can be monitored through Cacti's logging interface and optimized by adjusting the number of concurrent threads, poller cycle intervals, and timeouts for slow or unresponsive devices.

Data integrity and reliability in SNMP polling depend on stable network connectivity, proper device configuration, and realistic timeout settings. Missed polls or incorrect values may result from overloaded devices, incorrect community strings, or network segmentation. Cacti provides logging and debug options to track SNMP errors and polling failures, allowing administrators to take corrective action. Ensuring that time synchronization is in place on all monitored devices is also critical, as discrepancies can lead to inconsistent time-series data or skewed graph interpretations.

By mastering the use of SNMP and understanding how data sources function within Cacti, administrators can build a flexible, accurate, and scalable monitoring system that provides detailed insight into the health and performance of virtually any device in the network. This foundational knowledge supports the creation of comprehensive dashboards, meaningful alerts, and long-term trend analysis that drives proactive IT operations.

Chapter 4: Creating and Managing Graph Templates

Creating and managing graph templates in Cacti is a core part of streamlining the monitoring process, allowing administrators to apply consistent visualizations across multiple devices without having to define each graph manually. Graph templates in Cacti serve as blueprints that define how data should be presented visually, including which data sources to use, how graph items are arranged, what colors and line styles are applied, and how the vertical and horizontal axes are configured. This templating system is particularly useful in environments with many similar devices—such as switches, routers, servers, or storage systems—because it allows for efficient replication of monitoring configurations, ensuring standardization and reducing the risk of errors or inconsistencies.

The process of creating a graph template begins by accessing the Templates section of the Cacti web interface and choosing to add a new graph template. Each graph template requires a descriptive name that reflects the metric or purpose it will serve, such as "CPU Load," "Network Interface Traffic," or "Temperature Sensors." Once named, the template's core settings must be defined. These include specifying whether the template will allow multiple data sources, defining the default graph title format using placeholders like |host_description| or |data_query_title|, and configuring the lower and upper limits for the graph's vertical axis. These placeholders dynamically insert values at graph generation time, allowing a single template to generate unique titles per device or interface.

After setting general properties, the administrator defines the graph items, which are individual data lines or areas plotted on the graph. Each graph item is associated with a data source item and includes several attributes such as graph type (line, area, or stack), color (in hexadecimal format), GPRINT options (for displaying values like average, min, max, or last), and consolidation function (such as AVERAGE, MIN, or MAX). For example, in a network traffic graph, one graph item might represent inbound traffic as a green area while another represents outbound traffic as a blue line. Each graph item includes a sequence number that determines its rendering order, which affects how stacked areas or overlapping lines are displayed.

One of the most powerful aspects of graph templates is their integration with data templates and data input methods. A graph template does not function on its own—it requires a data template to provide the underlying data source structure. Data templates define how data is collected, including the step interval, heartbeat, data source type (gauge, counter, derive), and associated RRDTool settings. When a graph template is linked to a data template, it inherits the fields and variables defined in that template. This linkage allows Cacti to associate the correct RRD file paths and data source items with the visual components of the graph, enabling automation at scale.

To make graph templates more flexible, administrators can insert input fields and value templates that allow customization at graph creation time. These fields act as placeholders for values that may vary between devices, such as interface descriptions or SNMP indexes. When the graph is applied to a device, Cacti prompts the user to fill in these values or pulls them from the associated data query, automatically populating the graph with the appropriate context. This dynamic capability ensures that a single graph template can be reused across hundreds of instances while maintaining device-specific relevance.

Managing existing graph templates is an important part of system administration. Templates can be edited at any time to reflect changes in monitoring requirements, color standards, or layout preferences. When a template is modified, all graphs based on that template inherit the changes automatically unless they've been detached, meaning edited individually after creation. Cacti allows graphs to be locked to templates or managed independently, providing flexibility when exceptions are required. Administrators can also clone templates to create variants without starting from scratch, useful for testing alternative visualizations or applying different scaling techniques to the same dataset.

Exporting and importing templates enables the sharing of best practices between Cacti instances or among community members. Templates can be exported to XML files that include definitions for graphs, data templates, data input methods, and associated items. These XML files can then be imported into another Cacti installation using the Import Templates feature. This functionality makes it easy to deploy standardized monitoring across multiple networks or replicate proven templates across multiple environments. Many vendors and community contributors provide prebuilt templates for popular hardware and applications, saving time and ensuring coverage of all critical metrics.

Graph templates also support customization of legends, titles, and labels through RRDTool syntax. Users can define how numerical values are displayed, whether units are shown, and how grid lines or axis scaling behaves. For example, administrators might configure graphs to show bandwidth in bits per second, format large values using SI units, or display peak values with emphasized text. This level of control ensures that graphs are not only accurate but also easily interpretable by a variety of users, from technical staff to executives reviewing high-level reports.

In larger Cacti deployments, keeping graph templates organized is important for long-term maintenance. Cacti does not enforce a strict folder structure, but using consistent naming conventions—such as prefixes by device type, metric category, or location—can help simplify management. For example, templates might be named "Switch_Traffic," "Server_CPU_Load," or "Datacenter1_Uplink_Utilization." Documenting template purposes, associated devices, and configuration logic within the Cacti environment or external documentation also helps prevent confusion and accelerates onboarding of new administrators.

Automating the application of graph templates is made easier by combining them with device templates and graph automation rules. When a new device is added to Cacti and matched to a device template, the system can automatically assign predefined graph templates based on SNMP queries or manually defined attributes. This ensures that no critical metrics are missed during provisioning and that the monitoring environment remains consistent and scalable. As more devices are added and the infrastructure evolves, administrators can rely on graph templates to maintain uniform visibility across all systems.

Through careful design, effective use of data templates, and consistent management practices, graph templates become the foundation for scalable and meaningful monitoring in Cacti. They allow IT teams to visualize performance trends, identify issues quickly, and maintain high operational standards across diverse and growing networks. Whether used for bandwidth analysis, hardware health monitoring, or application performance tracking, graph templates provide the structure and automation necessary to turn raw data into actionable visual insight.

Chapter 5: Monitoring Network Devices and Interfaces

Monitoring network devices and interfaces with Cacti is one of the platform's primary strengths, enabling administrators to maintain visibility over the health, performance, and utilization of critical infrastructure components such as routers, switches, firewalls, load balancers, and wireless controllers. Cacti leverages the Simple Network Management Protocol (SNMP) to poll these devices at regular intervals, collecting numerical data about interface traffic, errors, discards, bandwidth utilization, and system status. By storing this data in round-robin databases and generating clear, customizable graphs, Cacti transforms raw metrics into visualizations that allow users to identify trends, detect bottlenecks, and respond proactively to anomalies across the network.

The process of monitoring begins by adding a new device through the Cacti web interface. The administrator specifies the IP address or hostname, SNMP version (v1, v2c, or v3), and credentials such as the community string for v1/v2c or the authentication and privacy settings for v3. Once the device is added, Cacti performs an SNMP query to gather system-level information and to verify that communication is functioning correctly. After successful detection, Cacti retrieves a list of available interfaces and their associated attributes, including interface index (ifIndex), description (ifDescr), type, speed, and operational status.

Each network interface on a device exposes multiple SNMP counters, such as ifInOctets, ifOutOctets, ifInErrors, and ifOutDiscards, which represent the total number of incoming and outgoing bytes, error frames, and discarded packets, respectively. These counters are incremented over time and must be processed as rates to derive meaningful metrics such as bits per second or packets per second. Cacti handles this transformation automatically by calculating the delta between polling intervals and adjusting for counter rollovers. The resulting values are then plotted on graphs that show traffic load over time, helping administrators detect congestion, diagnose anomalies, or identify underutilized links.

Graphing network interface data is typically handled through templates, which define how the collected SNMP data should be visualized. Templates standardize the appearance and layout of graphs, applying consistent styles for traffic lines, error markers, and labels. For example, inbound traffic may be shown as a green area and outbound traffic as a blue line, while interface errors could be displayed as red spikes. These visual conventions help users interpret data quickly and facilitate comparison across devices and interfaces. Cacti also supports the creation of multiple graphs per interface, such as one for traffic volume, one for packet rates, and another for errors, giving a comprehensive view of each interface's behavior.

Cacti's polling engine ensures that data is collected at regular intervals, typically every five minutes, which provides sufficient granularity for most operational use cases while maintaining performance. For networks that require closer monitoring or near real-time alerting, this interval can be reduced, although this places additional load on the poller and target devices. For high-density environments with hundreds or thousands of interfaces, switching from the default PHP-based poller to Spine—the high-performance C poller—improves scalability and reduces the likelihood of missed polling cycles or delayed data updates.

Device templates play a key role in simplifying the setup of network device monitoring. A device template can include a combination of data queries, graph templates, and SNMP OID mappings specific to a hardware platform or vendor. For example, a Cisco device template may include definitions for interface traffic, CPU utilization, and memory usage, while a Juniper template may focus on logical interfaces and routing table metrics. These templates can be applied to new devices automatically or manually, ensuring that all relevant metrics are consistently monitored and visualized without requiring repetitive configuration work for each individual device.

Interface monitoring in Cacti goes beyond just bandwidth usage. Administrators can also monitor interface status to detect link flaps or outages. The operational status (ifOperStatus) and administrative status (ifAdminStatus) of an interface can be polled and graphed or used in alerting logic. If an interface goes down unexpectedly, Cacti can generate a visual indication on the graph and, with the help of plugins or external tools, trigger alerts via email or other notification methods. This capability is essential for ensuring rapid response to critical network issues such as failed uplinks, misconfigured trunks, or cable faults.

In large environments, organizing devices and interfaces logically is important for ease of navigation and monitoring. Cacti provides the ability to group devices into categories such as by location, function, or customer, and graphs can be arranged into hierarchical trees to mirror the network's structure. For example, a graph tree might begin with the main data center, then branch into core switches, distribution switches, and access layer devices, each containing the associated interface graphs. This logical layout helps network operations teams find relevant graphs quickly and reduces the time needed to identify and diagnose issues.

Monitoring interfaces also supports capacity planning and resource optimization. By reviewing long-term usage trends, administrators can identify links that are consistently near saturation and plan for upgrades before performance issues arise. Conversely, links with low utilization might be candidates for downsizing or reassignment. Graphs that show peak traffic periods help in aligning maintenance windows or application deployment schedules to avoid disruption. Historical data also provides valuable context when investigating service degradation or evaluating the impact of network changes.

Custom data queries can be used to extend interface monitoring by including metrics not available through standard SNMP objects. These may include vendor-specific MIBs that provide enhanced visibility into queue depths, dropped packets, buffer utilization, or QoS policy performance. Cacti allows administrators to define custom SNMP OIDs and incorporate them into templates, making the monitoring framework adaptable to specialized or emerging technologies. By integrating these custom metrics into interface graphs, Cacti delivers deeper insight into the behavior of complex devices and the services they support.

With support for high-frequency polling, a flexible templating system, and comprehensive graphing capabilities, Cacti provides an effective and scalable solution for monitoring the interfaces that serve as the lifelines of any network. From small LAN environments to global enterprise infrastructures, Cacti enables visibility, accountability, and control over the flow of data across the network. Its ability to visualize performance over time, detect operational issues in real-time, and support proactive planning makes it a vital tool for modern network operations.

Chapter 6: Automating Device Discovery and Polling

Automating device discovery and polling in Cacti significantly enhances efficiency, consistency, and scalability across network monitoring environments by removing the manual steps traditionally required to identify, configure, and poll new devices. As network infrastructures grow in size and complexity, it becomes impractical for administrators to add and configure each device manually. Cacti provides built-in capabilities and plugins that allow for automatic detection of devices, pre-assignment of templates, and scheduling of polling tasks, which together streamline the onboarding process and ensure that data collection begins as soon as a device becomes active in the network.

The foundation of automated discovery in Cacti lies in the concept of network range scanning, where an IP address range or subnet is defined, and the system performs active queries to determine which devices are reachable and SNMP-enabled. This process often begins with a discovery rule that specifies the target network segment, SNMP version and credentials, and the type of devices being searched for. Using tools like ping, snmpget, or snmpwalk, Cacti sends probes to each IP address in the range to determine if a host responds and whether it supports SNMP. Devices that answer are then further queried to gather system information, such as hostname, system uptime, description, location, and interface inventory.

Once a device is discovered, Cacti can automatically classify it based on SNMP system object identifiers (sysObjectID), which correspond to specific vendor platforms or models.

For example, Cisco routers and switches, Juniper firewalls, and HP servers each report unique sysObjectIDs, which can be mapped to specific device templates within Cacti. This mapping allows the system to apply predefined monitoring configurations, including graph templates and data queries, without manual intervention. As a result, the newly discovered device can immediately begin feeding data into the Cacti system, producing traffic, CPU, memory, and availability graphs within minutes of detection.

To make discovery scalable and repeatable, administrators can schedule discovery jobs at regular intervals using Cacti's automation features. Scheduled scans ensure that new devices are detected shortly after being connected to the network, reducing the risk of blind spots in monitoring. For example, a discovery task might run every six hours to scan all access layer subnets, automatically detecting new switches added by the deployment team. As new devices are found, Cacti logs the discovery results, highlights differences between current and previous scans, and adds unmonitored devices to a staging area for administrator review or automatic inclusion.

Polling automation in Cacti is driven by the poller engine, which is responsible for executing data collection tasks at defined intervals. The poller reads the configuration for each device, queries the appropriate SNMP OIDs or script outputs, and updates the RRD files with fresh data. By default, the poller runs every five minutes, but this interval can be customized based on the needs of the environment and the capabilities of the monitored devices. For high-performance or large-scale deployments, the Spine poller is preferred due to its multithreaded design and optimized execution. Spine can handle thousands of devices and interfaces without introducing delays or missed polling cycles, making it ideal for use in automated monitoring workflows.

Poller configuration is critical in ensuring that the automation of data collection remains accurate and timely. Administrators must configure poller paths, execution frequencies, and maximum run times to match their infrastructure size and requirements. Devices that do not respond during a poller cycle are logged for follow-up, allowing teams to investigate outages or misconfigurations promptly. When integrated with alerting plugins, this polling data can trigger notifications or incident creation workflows, allowing network teams to respond quickly to issues detected during automated polling.

To further enhance automation, Cacti supports discovery and polling integration with network configuration management tools and orchestration platforms. For instance, when a new device is provisioned using Ansible or Puppet, a script can simultaneously register the device in Cacti using the CLI or API, assign it a device template, and trigger an initial poll. This creates a seamless, hands-off experience where monitoring is an inherent part of the deployment process rather than an afterthought. Similar integrations can be used with IP address management systems (IPAM), where a new IP allocation triggers a webhook that prompts Cacti to begin monitoring the assigned host.

Plugins like the Discovery Plugin and Autom8 offer additional automation features by providing graphical interfaces and more sophisticated rules for managing discovered devices. These tools allow for complex logic, such as assigning devices to categories based on IP range, device type, or naming conventions, and they support user-defined actions like enabling graph trees, applying location-based tags, or generating reports when new devices appear. This level of automation enables organizations to maintain a dynamic and accurate monitoring environment even as infrastructure rapidly changes.

Automation also supports the concept of configuration drift detection, where changes to devices are recognized automatically, such as when new interfaces are added to a switch or when SNMP configuration changes. Cacti can re-query the device, detect the new elements, and apply graph templates as needed to begin monitoring those components without requiring manual reconfiguration. This continuous adjustment ensures that monitoring coverage remains comprehensive and up-to-date even in highly fluid network environments.

By combining automated discovery with intelligent template assignment and efficient polling, Cacti allows administrators to scale their monitoring infrastructure to match the size and complexity of their organization's network. Automated polling ensures that all critical metrics are captured in a timely manner, while discovery ensures that nothing is missed when new hardware is introduced. These capabilities reduce the burden on IT staff, speed up operational readiness for new systems, and increase the overall reliability and responsiveness of the monitoring system. With proper configuration and the use of plugins and integrations, Cacti becomes a fully automated, intelligent monitoring platform capable of adapting to ever-changing infrastructure with minimal manual effort.

Chapter 7: Using Cacti Plugins for Extended Functionality

Using Cacti plugins for extended functionality allows administrators to transform a basic monitoring setup into a powerful and feature-rich network management system tailored to the unique needs of their environment. Cacti's plugin architecture is designed to be modular and lightweight, enabling users to selectively add features such as advanced user management, enhanced graphing tools, service-level monitoring, real-time status displays, syslog integration, and automated notifications without altering the core functionality of the platform. This modularity helps maintain system stability while offering flexibility to scale and adapt to growing operational demands.

The process of enabling plugin functionality in Cacti begins by installing the Plugin Architecture (PA) core system, which must be downloaded and placed within the Cacti installation directory. After installing and activating the plugin architecture from the console or web interface, Cacti provides a Plugins tab in the administration section where additional plugins can be uploaded, installed, and enabled. Once activated, each plugin adds new menus, tabs, or features to the Cacti interface and can be configured independently. Plugins can also define permissions, which allow administrators to control which users have access to their functionality based on roles and group assignments.

One of the most widely used plugins is the **Syslog plugin**, which adds a centralized syslog viewer to Cacti. This plugin listens for syslog messages sent from network devices and displays them in a searchable, filterable format within the

Cacti interface. By integrating syslog data with performance graphs, administrators can correlate log messages with network events, making it easier to investigate outages, security events, or misconfigurations. The syslog plugin supports severity-based filtering, keyword matching, and archival, allowing organizations to meet logging requirements without deploying a separate syslog server.

Another highly useful plugin is **THold**, short for Thresholds, which brings proactive monitoring and alerting to Cacti. With THold, users can define warning and critical thresholds for any monitored metric and configure Cacti to notify designated recipients via email or other channels when these thresholds are crossed. For example, if CPU utilization on a server exceeds 90% or if bandwidth usage on a WAN link spikes above expected levels, Cacti can automatically send an alert or flag the affected graph. THold supports static and dynamic thresholds and can trigger actions based on sustained conditions rather than momentary spikes, reducing false alarms and improving signal-to-noise ratio in alerting workflows.

The **RouterConfigs** plugin provides an interface for managing and backing up the configuration files of routers, switches, and firewalls. It works by connecting to devices via SSH or Telnet and issuing commands to retrieve their running configurations. These configs are stored in the Cacti database and can be compared across versions using built-in diffing tools. This allows network administrators to track changes, restore prior configurations, and detect unauthorized modifications, supporting both operational troubleshooting and compliance auditing.

For organizations with a large number of monitored devices, the **Autom8** plugin simplifies repetitive administrative tasks. Autom8 allows users to define rules that automatically assign templates, categories, or graph trees to new devices based on matching criteria such as IP range, hostname pattern, or sysObjectID. This streamlines onboarding and ensures consistency in monitoring configuration across devices of similar types. By applying standardized templates and rules, Autom8 helps eliminate configuration drift and reduces the time required to scale Cacti in expanding environments.

The **Monitor** plugin brings a real-time service check capability to Cacti, extending the platform's scope beyond SNMP-based polling. It enables the creation of checks for services such as HTTP, SMTP, DNS, FTP, and SSH, as well as custom port checks. Each check can be scheduled at regular intervals, and the results are recorded and displayed in status dashboards. This allows administrators to verify not only that devices are reachable but also that critical services are operational. Monitor integrates with other plugins like THold for alerting, creating a comprehensive monitoring solution that covers infrastructure, network traffic, and service availability.

Cacti also supports the **Boost** plugin, which enhances system performance by caching graph rendering and reducing load on the poller and database. In large environments where hundreds or thousands of graphs may be generated regularly, Boost significantly improves page load times and user responsiveness. It achieves this by storing pre-rendered graph images and only regenerating them when new data is available, reducing redundant processing and making dashboards faster to navigate.

For teams requiring role-based views and custom dashboards, the **Settings**, **Realtime**, and **SuperLinks** plugins offer fine-grained control over the user experience. Settings allows administrators to customize interface behavior, such as default time ranges, graph sizing, and navigation shortcuts. Realtime enables near-instantaneous graph updates, which are useful for live troubleshooting or when monitoring systems under stress. SuperLinks lets administrators create direct links between graphs and external tools or documentation, turning Cacti into a launchpad for incident response and diagnostics.

User management is another area where plugins provide valuable enhancements. The **User Admin** plugin adds functionality for managing groups, permissions, and authentication more efficiently. It can integrate with LDAP or Active Directory, enabling centralized user control and reducing the administrative overhead of managing credentials. Combined with per-plugin permission settings, administrators can ensure that users see only the data and tools relevant to their role, supporting security policies and simplifying the interface.

Plugins can be sourced from the official Cacti website or community forums, where developers share their work and provide installation instructions and usage guides. To maintain stability and security, plugins should always be tested in staging environments before deployment to production systems. Regular updates and compatibility checks with Cacti's core versions are also important, as plugins may rely on internal APIs or schema elements that change between releases.

Through careful selection and deployment of plugins, Cacti becomes far more than a simple graphing tool. It evolves into a full-featured monitoring and alerting solution capable of addressing the operational, security, and visibility needs of modern IT infrastructures. Each plugin adds a piece to the larger puzzle, enabling the platform to adapt to unique organizational needs while remaining lightweight and efficient.

Chapter 8: User Management and Permissions

User management and permissions in Cacti are essential for ensuring secure, organized, and role-appropriate access to monitoring data, administrative functions, and configuration interfaces. As Cacti is often used in environments with multiple users such as network administrators, systems engineers, helpdesk personnel, and auditors, its built-in role-based access control system plays a crucial role in maintaining operational boundaries and preventing unauthorized modifications. By creating and assigning user accounts with specific permissions, administrators can grant access to only the relevant sections of the platform based on each user's responsibilities, thereby enhancing security while supporting collaboration.

The user management process in Cacti begins by navigating to the User Management section within the web interface, where administrators can view existing accounts, create new users, and define or modify roles. Each user account in Cacti includes basic profile information such as username, full name, email address, password, and a primary user template or role. Users can be created manually through the interface or imported using LDAP or Active Directory integration, allowing large organizations to synchronize Cacti accounts with existing identity management infrastructure. This simplifies account provisioning and ensures consistency in credentials, password policies, and group memberships across systems.

Cacti's permissions model is based on a combination of user templates, user-specific overrides, and access lists. A **user template** serves as a reusable set of permissions that can be applied to multiple user accounts, streamlining the process of configuring access levels for different types of users. For example, a read-only user template might allow access to view graphs and dashboards but block the ability to modify devices or create alerts, while a network admin template may grant full access to SNMP device management, data sources, and graph templates. These templates not only define what users can do but also what they can see, including access to specific device trees, graph trees, and plugin features.

Within each user profile, Cacti provides detailed control over what elements of the system are visible and accessible. This includes options for viewing graphs, editing devices, managing templates, accessing logs, and using plugins. Permissions can be assigned globally or scoped to specific trees, graph groups, or data sources. For example, a helpdesk technician may be granted permission to view the access switch graphs for a specific building but be denied access to core router configurations or system logs. This granular access control supports separation of duties, compliance with security policies, and clear operational boundaries between teams.

In addition to permissions, Cacti allows for customized **graph viewing defaults** per user. Each user can have personalized settings that determine default time ranges, graph sizes, and navigation preferences. These settings make it easier for users to interact with Cacti in a way that suits their workflow, improving usability without affecting system-wide configurations. For instance, a security analyst might prefer 24-hour graph views to look for anomalies, while a network engineer might focus on week-long bandwidth trends to assess usage patterns.

LDAP and Active Directory integration further enhance user management by allowing Cacti to authenticate users against a centralized directory service. This is particularly valuable in enterprise environments where account management is centralized and compliance requires standard access controls. Cacti can be configured to bind to an LDAP server, perform group membership checks, and map users to roles automatically. This means that when a user is added to a specific LDAP group, Cacti can assign them the corresponding user template without manual intervention. If a user is removed from the group or their account is disabled in LDAP, they immediately lose access to Cacti, supporting strong account lifecycle management.

Password policies are another important aspect of user management. Cacti allows administrators to enforce password complexity requirements, minimum and maximum length, and expiration periods. Failed login attempts can be logged for audit purposes and tied to alerting systems for detection of brute-force attacks or compromised accounts. While Cacti's native authentication system handles these controls internally, external authentication sources like LDAP or SAML can offload password enforcement to corporate policy frameworks, further simplifying security compliance.

Activity auditing is supported through internal logging, which tracks actions taken by users such as logins, configuration changes, and graph or device edits. These logs are useful for troubleshooting, understanding user behavior, and supporting compliance audits. In environments with multiple administrators or distributed teams, knowing who made a specific change or when a device was added can be essential for maintaining operational transparency and accountability. Cacti's log files can be indexed like other data sources or exported to external logging platforms for centralized analysis.

Plugin permissions are also integrated into the user management system, allowing fine-tuned access control over features such as syslog viewers, configuration backup tools, or alert dashboards. Each plugin can define its own set of access rights, which are then applied through user templates or custom user settings. This ensures that users only see the plugins relevant to their responsibilities, avoiding confusion and reducing the risk of unauthorized actions. For example, only senior administrators might have access to the RouterConfigs plugin for downloading and restoring device configurations, while junior staff may only access the Syslog plugin in read-only mode.

Graph trees and device trees are also tied to permissions, giving administrators control over the visibility of specific monitoring data. Trees can be assigned to users or groups, ensuring that users only navigate through and view graphs for devices under their responsibility. This is particularly useful in managed service provider (MSP) scenarios, where each client should only see data related to their environment. Cacti supports multi-tenant setups through this mechanism, using graph tree assignments to isolate clients or departments from one another.

With careful configuration of user templates, roles, and permissions, Cacti enables organizations to maintain a secure and organized monitoring environment where every user has access to the tools and data they need—no more, no less. This balance of security and flexibility supports operational efficiency, reduces administrative overhead, and ensures compliance with access control policies across the entire monitoring infrastructure.

Chapter 9: Performance Tuning and Scalability Tips

Performance tuning and scalability in Cacti are critical for maintaining a responsive, stable, and efficient monitoring system, especially as the number of devices, interfaces, and users grows over time. Without proactive optimization, environments with hundreds or thousands of monitored elements can experience slow graph generation, delayed polling cycles, increased CPU and memory usage, and failed data collection. The first area to focus on when tuning Cacti is the **polling engine**, which handles the collection of data from devices and feeds it into RRD files for graphing. By default, Cacti uses a PHP-based poller, which is suitable for small to medium-sized environments, but for larger deployments, switching to **Spine**, the C-based multithreaded poller, offers substantial performance gains due to its ability to handle multiple polling operations simultaneously.

Installing and configuring Spine requires compiling it from source or using a prebuilt package and then enabling it within Cacti's settings. Once enabled, administrators can define the number of concurrent threads that Spine should use during each polling cycle. This thread count should be matched to the server's CPU capabilities, allowing parallel processing of data queries without overwhelming the system. The number of **polling threads** can be adjusted in the settings under the Poller tab, and it's advisable to increase this gradually while monitoring CPU load, poller logs, and the time taken to complete each cycle. If the polling interval is set to 300 seconds (5 minutes), it is essential that polling completes within that timeframe to prevent missed data points.

Another important area of optimization is **database performance**, as Cacti relies heavily on MySQL or MariaDB for storing device configurations, template data, user settings, and logging information. As the system scales, the size of the database increases, and without proper indexing, tuning, and maintenance, queries can become slower, affecting page load times and poller efficiency. Performance tuning begins with reviewing the database engine settings in the my.cnf or my.ini file, ensuring that InnoDB is used for all major tables, and configuring key parameters such as innodb_buffer_pool_size, query_cache_size, max_connections, and table_open_cache. The buffer pool should be large enough to keep frequently accessed data in memory, which significantly reduces disk I/O and speeds up response times.

Regularly optimizing and analyzing database tables is also necessary. Cacti includes a script that can be run periodically to optimize tables and remove overhead created by inserts and updates. Additionally, using a tool like mysqltuner can help administrators identify poorly performing queries or configuration bottlenecks. Enabling slow query logging in MySQL can also reveal which queries are taking too long and may need better indexing or adjustments in how data is being fetched and stored.

Graph rendering is another component that benefits from performance tuning. By default, Cacti generates graphs on the fly when users access the web interface, which can create performance issues when hundreds of graphs are requested simultaneously. Installing the **Boost plugin** provides a caching layer that pre-generates graph images and serves them from disk, drastically reducing load times and CPU usage. Boost allows administrators to configure cache lifetimes, generation intervals, and which graphs are cached, providing a flexible way to improve user experience and system responsiveness. It also helps reduce the load during peak access periods, such as daily checks or reporting hours.

As graph and data volume increases, **disk I/O** becomes a potential bottleneck, especially when many RRD files are updated every few minutes. Using solid-state drives (SSDs) for the RRD storage directory greatly improves write performance compared to traditional spinning disks. It's also important to separate the operating system, database, and RRD files onto different disks or partitions to reduce contention and improve parallel performance. Monitoring disk latency and queue depth helps identify whether the current storage setup is sufficient or needs to be upgraded.

Web server performance should not be neglected, as slow web responses can frustrate users and delay access to graphs and configuration tools. Apache or Nginx settings should be reviewed to optimize worker threads, timeouts, and caching. Using a PHP opcode cache such as **OPcache** helps reduce CPU load by keeping compiled PHP scripts in memory. If the environment uses SSL/TLS for secure access, enabling session reuse and compression can further reduce handshake times and data transfer size.

Cacti's internal logging and monitoring capabilities are helpful for tracking performance-related issues. The **poller log** records each polling cycle, showing total runtime, failed data queries, and completion status. The **system log** provides information about user actions, device errors, and plugin-related activity. Reviewing these logs regularly allows administrators to spot trends such as increasing poll times or unresponsive devices that may require attention. Devices with high response times or intermittent availability should be investigated and excluded from automated polling if they consistently degrade performance.

Reducing the number of unnecessary graphs and data sources also contributes to system efficiency. Templates should be applied only to relevant devices, and unused or obsolete graphs should be deleted to avoid wasting disk space and poller resources. Disabling verbose logging, limiting historical log retention, and pruning old RRD files that are no longer needed further optimize performance and reduce overhead.

In multi-user environments, applying **graph and tree permissions** helps avoid loading unnecessary data for users who only need access to specific devices or locations. This reduces the number of graphs queried at login or dashboard load time, easing the strain on both the database and web server. Using graph trees efficiently and keeping them logically organized also improves navigation speed and reduces backend processing during page rendering.

Finally, scaling out Cacti horizontally may be necessary for very large environments. This involves separating polling tasks across multiple servers, each with its own instance of Cacti or Spine, and consolidating graphs via remote data collection or using federated dashboards. While Cacti is not natively clustered, with careful planning, polling workloads can be distributed to balance the load and avoid bottlenecks. Combined with the right tuning practices, hardware optimization, and plugin usage, Cacti can remain responsive and reliable even under the demands of enterprise-scale monitoring.

Chapter 10: Common Issues and How to Fix Them

Common issues in Cacti environments can range from simple misconfigurations to deeper system-level problems that affect data polling, graph generation, performance, or user access, and understanding how to identify and fix them is crucial for maintaining a healthy and reliable monitoring system. One of the most frequently encountered issues is **missing or blank graphs**, which can occur for several reasons, including permission problems, incorrect data source associations, or polling failures. When a graph does not display any data, the first step is to verify that the corresponding data source is being updated. This can be done by viewing the "Data Sources" section and checking the "Last Updated" timestamp. If the timestamp is not recent or is blank, it means the poller has not successfully retrieved data.

To resolve blank graphs, administrators should confirm that the SNMP configuration on the target device is correct and that the community string, SNMP version, and access control settings allow polling from the Cacti server. Testing SNMP connectivity using tools like snmpwalk can help determine if the device is responding properly. If SNMP queries fail, the issue may be due to firewalls, incorrect community strings, or the SNMP service not running on the device. Once SNMP communication is restored, graphs should begin populating automatically at the next polling cycle.

Another common issue is **poller not completing on time**, which results in gaps in data or missed polls. This often occurs when the poller is overloaded due to a high number of devices, excessive threads, or insufficient system resources. Administrators should monitor the poller log and look for

196

entries indicating that the polling cycle took longer than the configured interval. If poller cycles are overlapping, it can cause performance degradation and lost data. Switching from the default PHP poller to **Spine**, the multithreaded C-based poller, often resolves this by significantly improving polling performance. Additionally, reducing the polling interval or the number of devices per poller run can help maintain cycle efficiency.

Problems with **graph rendering errors** can stem from file permission issues or misconfigured RRDTool paths. If graphs fail to render and return errors such as "broken image" or "cannot read RRD file," the system should be checked to ensure that the web server user (such as www-data or apache) has the correct read and write permissions on the rra directory and all RRD files. Also, verifying that the RRDTool binary path is correctly set in the Cacti settings is important, especially when using a custom or manually compiled version. Fixing permissions with commands like chown -R www-data:www-data /path/to/cacti/rra and chmod -R 755 often resolves these issues.

Login issues or inability to access the Cacti web interface are also commonly reported. These can result from forgotten passwords, locked accounts, expired sessions, or corrupted user configurations. If the administrator account is locked out, the password can be reset directly in the MySQL database using an SQL command such as UPDATE user_auth SET password=md5('newpassword') WHERE username='admin';. Ensuring the web server is running, the database is reachable, and the PHP session directory is writable are additional steps to take when dealing with login or session errors.

Slow page load times or system sluggishness may be caused by large graph trees, an overloaded MySQL database, excessive logging, or unoptimized templates. Admins should monitor the size of the poller_output and settings tables and consider truncating old log data to keep the database lean. Implementing the **Boost plugin** helps cache and pre-render graphs, reducing load during peak access times. Additionally, using a PHP opcode cache like OPcache and tuning Apache or Nginx settings for better performance can make the web interface more responsive.

Another frequent issue involves **device templates not applying correctly**, which results in graphs not being created or incorrect metrics being polled. This is often caused by mismatched SNMP OIDs or incorrect data query associations. Ensuring the correct sysObjectID is mapped in the device template and verifying that the device responds with expected OID values during discovery will prevent template mismatches. The SNMP Query Debug tool in Cacti can be used to simulate data collection and verify the results returned from the device.

RRD file corruption is rare but can occur if the system crashes during a write operation or if disk errors affect file integrity. When this happens, graphs may display strange values or error messages. The rrdtool info command can be used to inspect a suspected file, and corrupted files can sometimes be repaired using rrdtool dump and rrdtool restore commands. If repair is not possible, the data source and graph may need to be recreated, which results in loss of historical data but restores functionality.

Email alerts not being sent, especially when using plugins like THold, often trace back to misconfigured mail settings or missing system utilities like sendmail or postfix. Administrators should ensure that the mail transport agent is correctly installed and configured, that the "Mail/Alert Settings" in Cacti are properly set, and that the email format is correct. Testing alert delivery using a manual test event can help confirm that SMTP servers accept the connection and that messages are being sent.

Incorrect time zones or timestamps on graphs can lead to confusion, especially in global or multi-region deployments. Cacti uses the system time of the server, so verifying that the system clock is set correctly and synchronized using ntpd or chrony is essential. Additionally, the PHP and MySQL time zones should match the system time zone to prevent discrepancies in data collection and display. Time zone mismatches can lead to apparent gaps or misalignment in graphs.

When **plugins fail to load** or function incorrectly, it is often due to a mismatch between the plugin version and the core Cacti version. Before enabling a plugin, administrators should check compatibility and ensure the plugin directory has proper ownership and permissions. Plugin logs and the main Cacti log will usually show any fatal errors or missing dependencies. Updating plugins alongside core Cacti updates is good practice to avoid version conflicts.

By systematically diagnosing issues, reviewing logs, validating configurations, and using Cacti's built-in tools, administrators can resolve most common problems and keep the monitoring environment functioning smoothly. Keeping the system updated, regularly reviewing the logs, and applying best practices in permissions, performance, and template design reduces the frequency and impact of these common issues.

Conclusion

The journey through this book has explored the diverse landscape of network monitoring, showcasing the unique strengths and use cases of four powerful platforms—Zabbix, SolarWinds, Splunk, and Cacti. Each tool, while different in design, offers valuable capabilities that, when deployed strategically, help ensure visibility, stability, and performance across modern IT infrastructures.

In **Book 1: Mastering Zabbix**, we examined how a fully open-source solution can deliver enterprise-grade monitoring through flexibility, scalability, and automation. With Zabbix, organizations gain granular control over data collection, alerting, and visualization, making it ideal for proactive network management and long-term capacity planning.

Book 2: SolarWinds Unleashed provided a deep dive into one of the most widely adopted commercial platforms, emphasizing its intuitive interface and out-of-the-box integrations. Its robust feature set for infrastructure management, including configuration tracking, intelligent alerting, and performance monitoring, makes SolarWinds a compelling choice for enterprises seeking comprehensive, centralized control.

With **Book 3: Splunk Essentials**, we turned our attention to the world of machine data and real-time analytics. Splunk's powerful search language and flexibility in ingesting unstructured data open the door to advanced operational intelligence, security event management, and predictive analytics, transforming logs into actionable insights at scale.

In **Book 4: Cacti in Action**, we returned to the fundamentals of SNMP-driven monitoring and graphing, highlighting how a lightweight, open-source tool can provide reliable visibility into network health. Cacti excels in environments that value simplicity, customization, and clear visual reporting, and continues to be a trusted choice for many network administrators.

Across these four tools, one theme remains consistent—visibility is power. Whether you are monitoring devices, collecting metrics from cloud-native workloads, or analyzing machine-generated logs, the right tool not only alerts you to problems but also helps you understand, prevent, and respond to them effectively. No single platform fits all scenarios, and often, the most effective strategy involves blending multiple tools to match the unique challenges of your infrastructure. This book has equipped you with the foundational knowledge to make informed decisions, build efficient monitoring architectures, and evolve your practices in step with modern IT demands. As networks continue to grow in complexity and scale, your ability to observe, measure, and respond in real time becomes more important than ever. With the principles and tools covered in these pages, you are well-prepared to meet that challenge head-on.

www.ingramcontent.com/pod-product-compliance
Lightning Source LLC
Chambersburg PA
CBHW071245050326
40690CB00011B/2270